Sixty years a Yacht Designer

MAURICE GRIFFITHS
Sixty years a Yacht Designer

© Maurice Griffiths 1988

All rights reserved. Unauthorised
duplication contravenes applicable laws.

First published in Great Britain in 1988 by
Conway Maritime Press Ltd
24 Bride Lane, Fleet Street
London EC4 8DR

ISBN 085177 471 7

Typeset by MJL Ltd, Hitchin, Herts.
Printed by Richard Clay Ltd, Chichester,
and bound by The Bath Press Ltd.

CONTENTS

Chapter I	1
II	9
III	19
IV	28
V	38
Seaway	47
Ionia	49
Wild Lone II	51
Lone Gull I	54
Juliana	57
Centreboards	60
Solani	66
Tinka	69
Tarmaris	72
Jeanne D'Arc	76
Kismet	78
Lone Gull II	82
Tidewater	87
Good Hope	91
Golden Hind	96
Idle Duck	100
Kylix	104
Noontide	108
Gulf Stream	111
Bay Class Yachts	114
Appendix, Taking off a Boat Lines	117

I

What causes a man to take up a certain interest, an unusual hobby or activity perhaps, and become absorbed by it for the rest of his life has long been debated. Some experience in early childhood, for example, has been known to set off the spark of interest which might grow to an obsession in manhood.

The first sight and sounds of railway trains when I was four certainly implanted in me a love for railways in all their forms which has remained with me ever since. Both born in London, my elder brother and I were taken by our parents to live in Ipswich as a centre for my father's business as a glove salesman. The windows of our house looked across a small park to the main line of the Great Eastern Railway, and the trains with their beautiful blue engines with shining brass and flashing red side rods captured a small boy's imagination shared by all his neighbouring pals.

But before I went to school at the other end of the town — an ancient establishment where Thomas Wolsey, destined to become a Cardinal to Henry VIII, had once been a pupil — we had also discovered the excitement of the docks. Here, in those days at the head of the river Orwell, the great wet dock was to be found crowded with shipping. Along the quays we could always find small coasting steamers, often a rusty vessel listing under a great deckload from the Baltic unloading at Brown's timber wharf, and invariably a dirty collier discharging her coal by dust-spilling grabs at Gas Works quay. There were rows of Thames barges against Paul's and Fison's wharves, or underway with their brown sails coming in or out through the lock gates on every tide. But there would also be two, and sometimes three or four, weather stained square riggers with yards cockbilled, unloading their nitrate or grain cargoes or whatever, hailing from half way round the world.

The Docks were a paradise of adventure for small boys, which for me at least was enhanced by the noisy dock engine bashing a line of trucks along the quay and smelling of steam and coal smoke and hot engine oil. Outside the lock gates and beyond Orvis's barge yard, however, lay an even more exciting attraction. Under the shadow of Cobbold's Brewery in a bight of the river a number of small craft, perhaps twenty or more, rode to their moorings.

It was the sight of these little vessels, most of them shabby nondescript converted ships' boats with hutchlike cabin roofs, or ancient straight stem cutters with grotesquely long bowsprits, that fired our imagination and, for me at least, sowed a seed of what could only be called sea fever. Two of the better looking boats in the anchorage always took my fancy: one was a cutter of about 6 tons with straight stem and a graceful counter stern, named *Undine*, which I at once began to covet: the other was a fine sturdy cutter with a separate topmast, almost knee-high bulwarks running round her decks, and great beam with her name *Scoter* on her transom stern. I was not to know as I gazed on these two favourites that my pal, Claude, and I would one day own *Undine*, nor that the bigger *Scoter* would eventually have considerable influence on my designs.

One of the many interests of my mother, well read and gifted with an impelling desire for knowledge outside the normal duties of the home, was the study of astrology — in addition to periods devoted to astronomy, theosophy and, to my father's explosive anger, the Suffragette Movement. After studying my horoscope Lena always maintained that, having been born in May under the sign of Gemini, I should find myself pursuing two separate interests throughout my life. Apart from my unrelated devotion to railways and the sea and ships, looking back over the years it really has been significant how often I have found myself engrossed in two entirely different activities, projects or interests at the same time. And thus I have been able to regain vigour, recuperate energy when weary of working on one subject, by turning to the other.

While still at school, Claude, who lived a few doors away, joined forces with me in building up a Gauge 1 model railway which in time filled an attic room and the landing in our house. Doing odd jobs for the cash, and saving every penny of our joint pocket money (even foregoing sweets) we bought the scale track and clockwork and steam locomotives on the secondhand market. Everything else, stations, signals, level crossings, bridges, coaches and wagons we made ourselves, finding it all an absorbing hobby which kept us both out of mischief — most of the time. My brother, seven years my senior, was not involved for he had emigrated to Canada to seek an ever elusive fortune.

When the fuelless, hungry and bleak years of 1914-18 war were over, and Claude and I had both left school, he joined his father's business in the town while my hopes of being apprenticed to the Great Eastern locomotive works were dashed, for the premium could not be found as father was 'temporarily embarrassed financially': a state which was to have hard repercussions later on. Meanwhile, I managed to get a job as junior in an estate agent's office, thankful to be working in an interesting business, and even earning a small wage.

Our enthusiasm for miniature trains was on the wane, for Claude already shared with me a growing interest in sailing a boat of our own, and the following spring we took our week's summer holiday hiring *Reindeer*, a 24-foot sloop on the Norfolk Broads. There were few yachts to be seen so soon after the war (only two motor cruisers passed us), but the reed lined rivers and broads were as lovely and peaceful as the photographs in the old Great Eastern carriages showed them, and dozens of windmills were still at work draining the marshes. Despite the tangles and humiliations we got ourselves into, nothing cured us of our ardour to get a boat, a real yacht, of our own.

The railway was taken up and sold piecemeal (what collectors' pieces those old Bassett-Lowke engines would be now) and on learning that the white cutter, *Undine*, which we had admired so often, was on the market at a price we could not afford, we put in an offer which was accepted with suspicious haste, and had the yacht put on the hard for the customary survey.

Undine *our first boat, looked splendid bowling along, but...*
...too often it ended like this.

Not knowing how to carry out an inspection, indeed what defects to look for when one's eyes are blinded with yearning and love, we decided she was wholly beautiful and sound, paid over our seventy pound notes and waited for the tide to float her and allow us to assume command, too bewildered to say very much. Our ship was a typical straight stem cutter of the 1870s, full in the bows and fine under the counter, a classic codshead-mackerel-tail type, 30 feet in length with an eyecatching sheer and traditionally 'long in the leg' with 5-foot 3-inch draft. We were to curse that deep draft before we were through with her, or she with us.

We soon discovered that *Undine* was a handful for two beginners and could not be made to twist and turn from one tack to the other with a flick of the helm as our *Reindeer* had on the Broads. It took us many trials to learn how a deep boat with a long straight keel needs sailing round steadily with little helm and brought through the wind's eye with the forestays'l held aback. Thus, with anxious hearts and dry throats we missed stays until inevitably we ploughed onto the mud flats while the tide left us to lie over on our bilge at an angle of fifty degrees.

Many hours of that wonderfully hot summer of 1921 did we spend enduring the discomfort of lying aground while the world seemed to pass us by, debating just why it was that yachts had to have such deep draft and such sharp bottoms. After all, we had noticed, the hundreds of spritty barges we saw working up and down the river with their cargoes had no keels: they were quite flat bottomed and sat fair and square on the hard at Pin Mill. Yet we knew they made their coastal passages from London River and the Medway to ports all round the coast, from the Wash to the West Country.

We were to learn in time that on the Crouch, along the Southend foreshore and in the Medway and at West Mersea there were miniature barges: little barge yachts with flat bottoms and leeboards in sizes from 22 foot to 45 foot or so, the smaller ones generally rigged as gaff sloops with the foresail on a wooden roller. The small barge yacht had been originally introduced on the Crouch by E B Tredwen in the early 1890s when Burnham was rapidly becoming the Londoner's popular anchorage after the Great Eastern Railway had reached the town with its branch to Southminster.

At the end of the season *Undine* was sold, Claude joined another syndicate with a smack, and I began at weekends scouring the anchorages around the coast on my bike in search for a small centreboarder or one of the little barge yachts. Between Paglesham and Fambridge on the Crouch north to Woodbridge and Orford there seemed nothing for sale of the shallow draft type I was looking for: it appeared that boatbuilders rarely built boats of this type.

In the end I settled for a 17-foot ship's boat with lifting cabin top and mast in a tabernacle which had been converted during the war for hiring out on the Broads. *Dabchick* was not ideal — she was all I could find within my limit of forty pounds — but I found I could manage her alone with ease, and she taught me a lot that season during weekends and a week's cruising exploring all the rivers and creeks between the Deben and the Roach.

A slump in house property about this time resulted in Griffiths, on the principle of 'last in first out', getting the push from the office. Attempts to find a job in the general air of unemployment in the town proved fruitless, and in order to find something constructive to do I started a small yacht selling agency. There were then no yacht brokers in Suffolk, and I managed to build up connections with one or two of the London firms. This began to bring in a scratch living (it reminded me of fowls

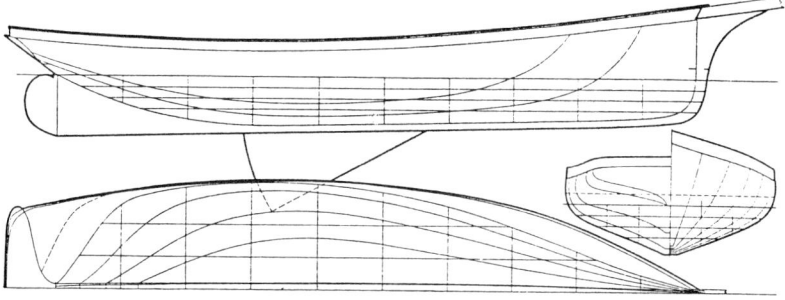

American centreboard racers. The lines of Arrow, *built in 1875, show an early form with fine bow lines and extremely full quarters. This sloop was 61.8 feet on the waterline with 20.2 feet beam and drew 5.5 feet.*

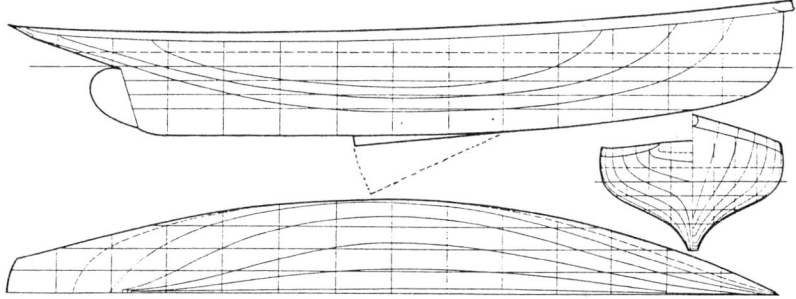

Puritan, *a later 'compromise type' built in 1885, with a deeper hull and outside ballast, and a finer run up into the counter. With LOA of 93 feet and 81.1 feet WL, the draft is 8.5 feet with 27 tons of lead on the keel.*

scratching in a farmyard), but also plenty of experience of good and bad yachts.

Unable to pay for laying up *Dabchick* at the end of the season I sold her at a small profit and found a badly run down 24-foot centreboard sloop of a type I had been looking for. She taught me some of the faults of a badly constructed centreboard case and an ill-conceived plate and the troubles that can accrue, and set me thinking how these things could be improved with forethought. Boatless again the next winter, I shared for a time another centreboarder, a 22-foot racing sloop, with a keen and adventurous shipmate, until falling for a pretty little 26-foot barge yacht with steel leeboards working through slots in the chines in cases inside the topsides.

None of these boats had an engine — few yachts under 32 feet or so did sport what was called 'an auxiliary motor' in those days — and we had to learn sailing, seamanship, boatmanship, picking up moorings, anchoring, laying out a kedge and hauling off, using the sweep (a long springy oar) as the bargemen did in a calm, and always the importance of working tides, making tides your friends, the hard way. There were no sailing schools, no classes at yacht clubs, no courses in sailing or boat building at universities. Except for the few with salt in their blood, boat sailing and cruising around the coast was an unknown activity to the majority of people.

From various books the lending library managed to find for me I read that the idea of a centreboard, or drop keel, had come originally from America, the invention in Colonial days of a US naval lieutenant. With large areas of shallow waters along their east coast, such as Barnegat and Chesapeake Bays, the Yankee boat builders for almost two centuries had accordingly been building shallow draft fishing boats and coasting schooners up to 200 tons with large wooden centreboards. American yachtsmen had soon cottoned on to this useful contrivance and developed broad, shallow, fast yachts for racing. Indeed, even the early defenders of the America's Cup during the 1870s and 1880s were broad beamed centreboard schooners and sloops, which proved their racing superiority over the narrow and very deep English cutters.

Just why the yacht builders in Great Britain should have clung so doggedly to this deep hull form, I read, was the result of their copying the fastest vessels they knew, namely the Revenue cutters and the naval fly boats with their enormous spreads of canvas. So it was that when racing was introduced — which meant multi-guinea wagers for matches between sporty noblemen — the shape and rig of most of the yachts taking part followed a similar pattern. In old engravings of early Victorian yacht races the vessels look as much alike as many of our present day plastic sloops.

Because of this uniformity in a yacht racing fleet — except for size which could vary from a 'little one' of 40 tons up to 200 tons or so — the Royal Thames Yacht Club in 1854 introduced a simple rating formula for handicapping which the club's official measurer could carry out on the deck of each boat without the need to go below. Based on the ancient Builders' Tonnage Measurement for merchant vessels, it measured merely the length from stemhead to the after side of rudder post, disregarding any overhang at the stern together with the main breadth, or beam. Expressed as $\dfrac{L - B(B \times \frac{1}{2}B)}{94}$ it gave the Thames Yacht Measurement for race handicapping. The fact that for the next hundred years yachts in Britain were familiarly known by their TM tonnage was an indication of the conservative nature of yachtsmen. It is debatable, however, whether the present fashion of describing a yacht's size by her length on deck in feet or metres is any more accurate in assessing her bulk or displacement. Some of the effects that this TM Rule was to have on yacht design will be discussed in a later chapter.

The yacht agency business in Ipswich scarcely brought in a living, and I had started to write articles for railway magazines, local papers and one or two of the yachting weeklies which were published in London. A lift up was to be asked to write a regular column in a weekly called the *Yacht Owner*, and this encouraged the idea that I might be all set for a career in journalism.

Meanwhile, having parted with my cranky little barge yacht, I came across lying for sale in the saltings at West Mersea what appeared at once the kind of boat to suit my way of cruising. She was a small black cutter called *Storm*, with straight stem and transom stern, said to be 24 feet on deck with a fine beam of 9 feet.

Built at Leigh-on-Sea in 1910, she was on the lines of a miniature bawley, and after my previous boats her cabin seemed enormous, with standing headroom (well, with head bent) under the large skylight. Furthermore, with all her iron ballast inside she drew only 3 feet 3 inches, an ideal shape and draft for my kind of crusiing. And for the first time I was to have a boat with an auxiliary motor. This was admittedly a primitive piece of mechanism compared with today's sophisticated installations, a one-lung 3½ horsepower Kelvin which warmed up on petrol and ran on paraffin (kerosene). It had neither clutch nor reverse gear, and handling the boat under power in tight spots, I was to learn later, needed care and judgement, as under sail, and with the caution learnt with my previous boats I still carried a sweep along the rail with its blade tucked between the after shroud lanyards, despite the presence of what the Dutch call the *hulp motor*.

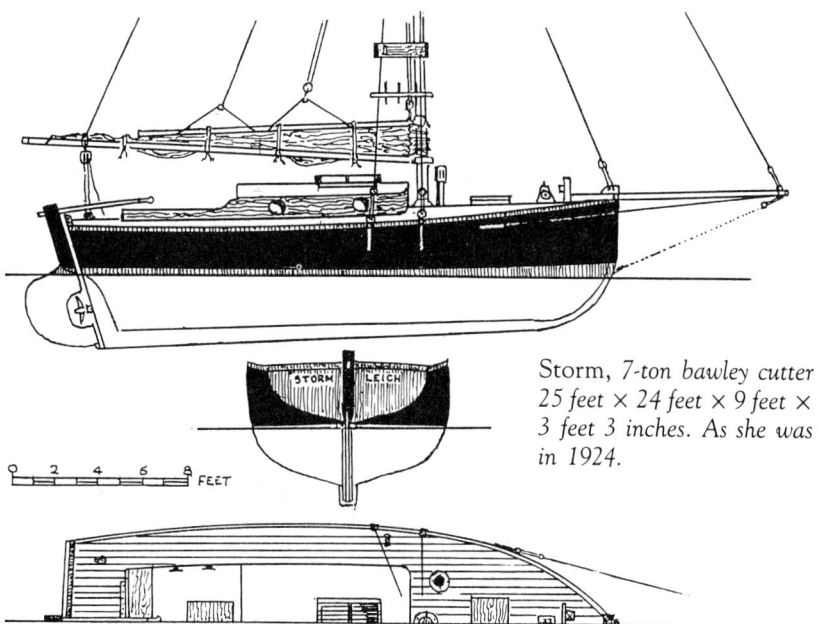

Storm, *7-ton bawley cutter 25 feet × 24 feet × 9 feet × 3 feet 3 inches. As she was in 1924.*

Storm proved the most satisfactory of my first five boats, for she would sail herself with tiller held by line for hours, and lie quietly when hove-to with mains'l eased a little, forestays'l backed and helm alee. Like many of the traditional straight stem type with long straight keels she could pull hard on the helm when closehauled in a breeze, and on these occasions she taught me the value of rigging tiller lines, one from each side of the cockpit coamings long enough to pass once, or twice if necessary, round the end of the tiller, which gave a two-to-one purchase on the helm and relieved all that arm stretching. Tiller lines are useful, too, for keeping the rudder quiet at night, or giving the boat a sheer in the tide. With today's high-tech approach to sailing, of course, you can have the same service operated for you by a variety of expensive electric tiller controllers, more sophisticated and sensitive than the humble cord — so long as the batteries do not run out.

With the experience I had now accumulated, and with the confidence of youth, I thought (repeat, *thought*) I knew enough to write a useful little book on sailing aimed at 'the man in the street'. I felt there was a need to show the uninitiated how to start with an inexpensive cabin boat, like a converted ship's boat, an elderly cutter or yawl, for well under £100; how to maintain it, handle it under sail, choose an anchorage, pick up moorings, in fact learn simple boatmanship, and how it could all be managed on a proverbial shoestring. After all, I had been doing just that for the previous four years.

The book, *Yachting on a Small Income* (a provocative enough title for 1924) was accepted by Edward Arnold in London, who arranged to publish it on their spring list. Like all young authors I found waiting for my first effort to burst on the world very trying. But before the year was out an event occurred which threw other responsibilities onto the budding author.

The sudden death of my father in his fifties revealed a sorry state of affairs, which resulted in our house and furniture being sold up to meet the demands of the creditors. My elder brother lived far away with a wife and child and could not help. Our mother went to live with her widowed sister in Lincolnshire, and *Storm* had to go for the money to be put to immediate necessities. But I vowed I would buy her back some day if and when I could afford her again.

Prospects in Ipswich of finding a job for an untrained young fellow in a time of much unemployment seemed bleak. Banking on my slight contacts through press articles and the hoped-for royalties from my book, I took the bull by the horns and moved up to London, my real home town. With the determination to make some sort of living as a freelance writer I became another of the anonymous 'bed sit' community, prepared to face the immediate future far removed from sailing.

II

The months that followed were predictably coloured with anxiety, loneliness and an unwelcome collection of rejection slips from editors. The Press was proving a hard nut to crack, and to add to these disappointments, after a few months the regular standby, my column in the *Yacht Owner*, ceased as the paper folded up and there was nothing left to pay its contributors.

A ray of light appeared as *Yachting on a Small Income* was published in April, a small enough volume for all the work put into it, priced at 4s 6d (22p). At the customary royalty of 10 per cent there was to be no fortune involved, and I found I had to wait for six months to receive the second cheque, but the publishers assured me that, for a yachting book, it was selling in encouraging numbers. In the meantime I had managed to place a few more articles and stories in various weeklies and monthly magazines which were still being published in those pre-radio days.

The prospect of a second winter, however, continuing to struggle alone in a bleak bed-sitter looked very distasteful, and I was about to accept an offer through a yacht broker friend to join the delivery crew of a motor yacht which was bound through the canals to the South of France, for the sake of the cash and the experience. But out of the blue a letter arrived from one George Bittles, the manager of a newly launched yacht brokerage fortnightly called *Yacht Sales and Charters*, asking me to call and see him.

Bittles explained that he had picked up a copy of my book from a news stand and decided its author, if he was free, might be the kind of editor he needed to help run his paper. I almost cried out 'Oh yes, I'm *free!*' but managed to keep calm and agreed to start in the office the very next day.

Beneath the eighteenth-century offices of the old *Saturday Review* in King Street, Covent Garden, our room was a medley of papers, galley proofs, photographs, file boxes, books, stationery and zinco blocks smelling of printers ink. It was shared with Bittles and a shorthand typist, and it was the start of an exciting occupation that has held me all these years. And the unexpected elevation from the lonesome anxieties of a freelance writer to a challenging job in the friendly atmosphere of a warm office with a desk of my own was so great that I never, never forgot it; and in silence I blessed that first little book venture of mine and what it had brought me.

Yachts Sales and Charters had been launched as Bittles's own idea of a money spinner and as an offshoot from the much older but ailing *Yachting Monthly*, whose offices were on the next floor under the *Review*'s ownership. Our editorial pages were flanked each side by columns of classified advertisements for yachts for sale and charter, arranged under headings like Sloops, Cutters, Yawls, Schooners, Motor Yachts and, yes, even Steam Yachts, and illustrated by small photoblocks. The pages could be a delight for the dreamer or the connoisseur of yachts.

Editing this fortnightly became pure joy for me, for although I had everything about an editor's duties and responsibilities still to learn, from what I had already learnt from boats and in writing my book I felt I had a good idea of what the less wealthy yachtsman, the man-in-the-street with the sea in his blood, was really wanting in a yachting paper. And before long increasing print order and sales figures began to bear this out, while on the next floor those of the parent monthly, concerning itself almost entirely with big class racing, Cowes society events and the yacht clubs, were fast dropping back. It was a hectic and exciting time, for Bittles had his hands full with managing the brokerage side while our typist was flooded with letters from readers, yacht owners and their agents. I was glad I could type my own letters and editorials.

Within a year our proprietor had grown tired of the losses on the monthly, and its elderly editor was asked to resign (such affairs were less brutally conducted in those days). *Yacht Sales and Charters* was absorbed by the *Yachting Monthly*, and I was appointed its editor at the end of 1926 with a gratifying increase in salary. And over the next forty one years (with a break only for naval experiences between 1939 and 1945) I remained in the chair until retirement in 1967.

Features on cruising yacht designs and descriptions from the board of well known designers, such as Linton Hope, Norman Dallimore, Morgan Giles, Albert Strange, E P Hart, A R Luke, A E Payne, A Westmacott, Harrison Butler and others, proved to be highly popular with our readers. This led to our holding design competitions in which readers with ideas of their own were able to show their talent. For some time I had become addicted to sketching out lines of boats on any scrap paper to hand, and had found that trying to make a proper design of even a little yacht demanded a good deal of imagination and patience if the result was to be a vessel that would not only float somewhere as designed, but would also sail and handle as she was intended. Fully addicted to the doodling habit I began to study all designers' plans that I could find, and searched the libraries for books on the subject.

Happily for me a well known designer of a whole range of beautiful yachts in the years before and after the First World War was still in practice in an office in Piccadilly, a short walk from King Street. Fredk. Shepherd, as he always signed himself, a Member of the Institution of Naval Architects and noted for the graceful sheer, well balanced bows and counter sterns of his designs ranging from 5 and 8 tons TM up to a beautiful schooner of 100 tons, was kind hearted and helpful towards an aspiring young fellow. Through his generosity I was invited to come to his drawing office any time I could get away and see how things were done, and thus I was able to grasp the need for accurate drawing, an appreciation of hull form from a set of lines, to learn the patience necessary to work out all the calculations of weights and areas involved, and how to draw sweeping curves which were fair and not faintly warped. I thus owed much in my prentice days of boat designing to Fredk. Shepherd, who later retired to his Hampshire home to live to the ripe old age of one hundred.

After making a number of abortive attempts to draw out the designs of the type of shallow draft boat that appealed to me, I received a request for just such a design from the owner of a large ketch which he kept on the Hamble river and which drew all of eight feet. My client wanted a small centreboarder 28 feet or so overall but with a nearly flat bottom for sitting upright on the mud, which he intended to use for wildfowling during the winter when his other yacht was laid up. She was to have a comfortable cabin for two wildfowlers and their guns, a coal range for warmth, a snug gaff cutter rig, and an auxiliary motor for working up to the head of creeks.

The result was a carvel hull not unlike a blown up dinghy's, with 8.7 feet beam and drawing 2.5 feet only with the centreplate and rudder plate hauled up. The mast was stepped in a wooden tabernacle well aft so that the plate (of $\frac{3}{8}$ inch steel and L-shaped like an open knife blade) could work through a slot in the foredeck with its tackle led aft to the cockpit, leaving the cabin almost free of the case. With only a five inch deep outside iron ballast keel to keep her stable in blowy weather, she would take the ground like the 'sitting duck' I thought to call her. But the owner said he didn't care for an Indian chief's name for her, and chose *Wind Song* when she was launched at Feltham's yard in Portsmouth in 1929.

This little boat turned out a distinct success, not only as a wildfowler but as a capable and versatile little cruising yacht in the choppy Solent waters and later off the East Coast; and thanks to her rugged all-teak construction she is still (1987) afloat, now Bermuda cutter rigged and with her third engine, a small diesel.

This was followed shortly afterwards by an order from a keen ornithologist for a centreboarder suitable for lying at a mooring which dried out on the sands inside Holy Island off the Northumberland coast, where he studied the wild birdlife. By request she was to have a Fifie-type pointed stern and as *Loon* (the Great Northern Diver) she was splendidly built, mainly of teak, in 1930 by Millers of St Monance, Fife. Gaff cutter rigged her length was 30 feet on deck with 9 feet beam, and drawing just under 3 feet she had the same style of L-shaped centreplate as *Wind Song*'s. She is still sailing and based in Faversham on the north Kent coast.

Whilst the arrangement of the L-shaped centreplates in these two yachts worked easily and took up little room above the cabin sole, it was found that the leading edge of the plate when fully lowered was forward of the centre of effort (CE) of the sail plan, which was enough to cause the yacht to gripe, to try to slew up into the wind. Although this gave her a determined 'bite' to windward, in breezy weather she needed fairly heavy weather helm to hold her — certainly a need for tiller lines. With this in mind I began to study all the centreboard designs I could find in books on American yachts and work boats, and learnt all I could gather on the habits of centreboarders.

This is not to imply that I was obsessed with the centreboard type of cruising boat to the exclusion of all others, for over the years I came to design a fairly wide variety of types to suit owners' requirements. *Storm*'s bawley type form certainly influenced my ideas for the simple shoal draft fixed keel type, for I managed to produce a series of transom sterned cutters, with snug rigs and short bowsprits with Wykeham Martin roller furling jibs, in sizes from 25 feet to 30 feet on deck, and iron ballast keels giving a draft from 3 foot 3 inches to 4 feet 3 inches, which were to the orders of various clients.

My research took me into the realms of American magazine articles and owners' stories concerning their claims that a good shallow draft yacht, with good beam with or without a centreboard, could in extreme conditions at sea prove safer for its crew than the so-called English type of deep, narrow heavy displacement yacht. I came across various accounts where deep keeled vessels, when hove-to or lying ahull under bare poles, had been constantly swept and suffered severe damage by the seas. Lying like a half-tide rock in the water the yacht with its immense lateral resistance could not 'give' to the seas and suffered accordingly. In some cases the yacht was overwhelmed and the mast burst out of her, as in the case of Sinclair's small Falmouth quay punt *Joan* in the North Atlantic. Later on were cases of deep and heavy yachts running before storm force winds being pitchpoled, driving their bows deep while their sterns were lifted by a following sea, and turning end over end. The Colin Archer ketch *Sandefjord* was, I think, the first to be reported, while years later Miles Smeeton's *Tzu Hang*, a lean and deep double ender, distinguished herself by pitchpoling on two occasions when rounding Cape Horn as recorded in *Once is Enough* by Miles Smeeton.

Following this fascinating research of the varied behaviour in heavy weather conditions of different types of yacht, I had much correspondence with the designers and owners of

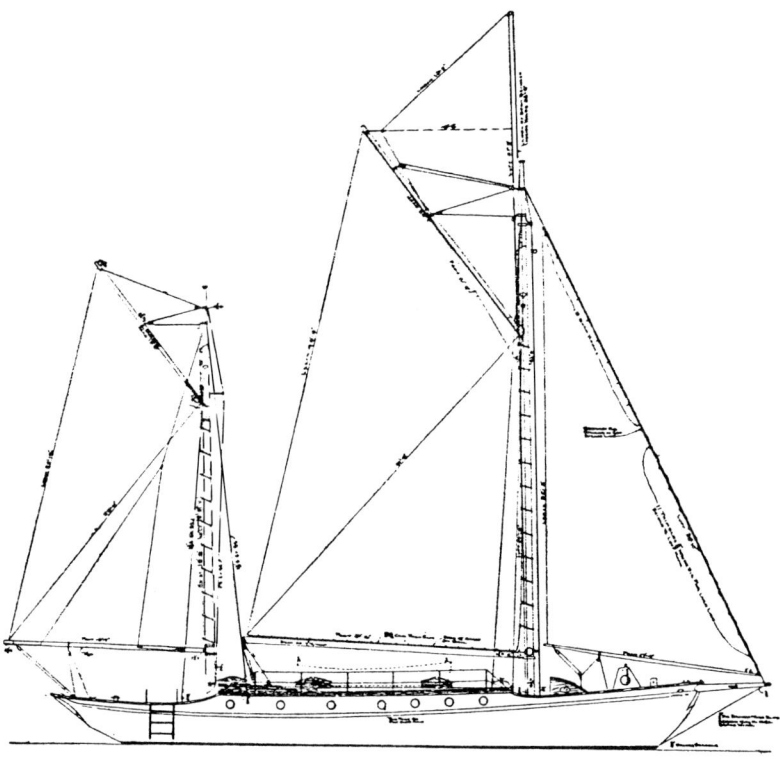

Alice, *52-foot centreboard ketch.*

American shoal draft yachts which had come through hair raising conditions off their eastern seaboard. Let me quote just one of them, from the late Henry Howard who had designed with Commodore Ralph M Munroe, an authority on United States lifeboat design and shallow draft yachts, a 52-foot ketch *Alice*, 44 feet on the waterline and with 13 feet 7 inches beam. Her draft was just four feet with the large wooden board raised, and during a heavy blow Howard described how his ship lay ahull without warps or sea anchor streamed, sidling down the face of the oncoming seas which broke in the slick or smooth she was leaving to windward of her. While swept with fine spray most of the time, the *Alice* was at no time rough handled by the seas which seemed, as Howard wrote, as though they could not get hold of her. It must be remembered, however, that for a centreboarder to survive in such conditions she must have plenty of sea room, many miles, to leeward of her: no cruel lee shore in sight.

An opportunity came my way soon after to try my hand at another shallow draft cruising yacht. It was the largest order I had received so far and, bearing in mind my short experience of yacht designing to date, I found this quite a challenge. The Commodore of the Royal Egypt Yacht Club called at my office and explained that he wanted a large seagoing centreboarder in which he and his friends could cruise

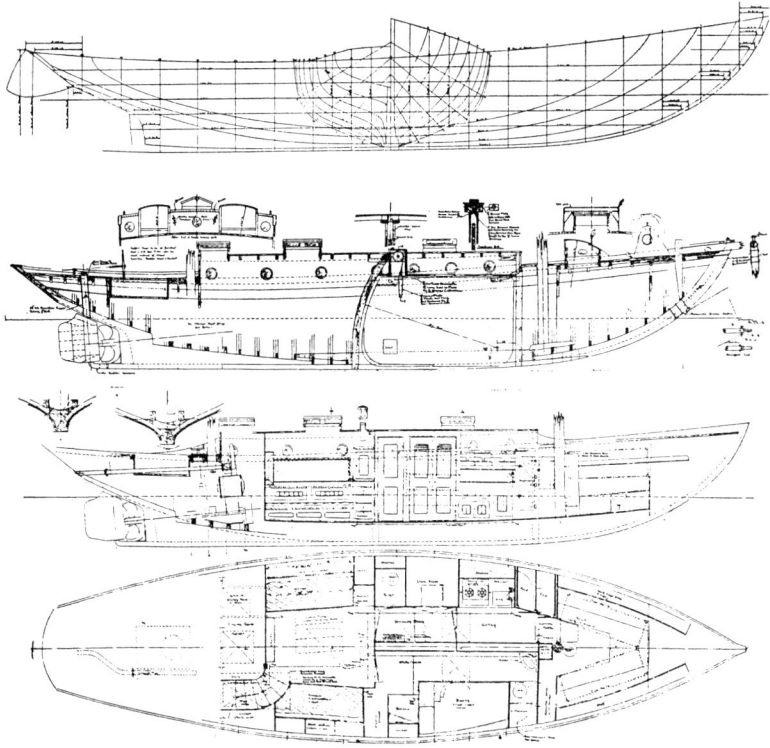

Plans of Henry Howard's centreboarder show her light draft of 4 feet on a 44-foot WL, and the arrangement of the barn door type centreboard.

comfortably around the Greek Islands and Ionian Sea; but at the same time the hull draft must not exceed four feet, as he also was planning a cruise up the Nile, where he had archaeological interests below the First Cataract. He stressed that he wanted a reasonably fast boat, easy to handle with his two Egyptian crew, and she was to have his favourite caique type pointed stern, to have no motor ('can't bear the smell of the things in our hot climate') and she must be well balanced so as to have tiller steering, no wheel.

This yacht turned out to be 45.5 feet long on deck with just over 13 feet beam, which enabled me to place the centreboard nicely admidships in balance with the centre of lateral resistance (the midpoint of the immersed hull profile) in relation to the centre of effort (CE) of the ketch sail plan. The board was a barndoor affair built up of hardwood planks lightly weighted to make it sink, and reaching up to the deckhead. When lowered it drew eight feet, and the case nicely divided two sleeping cabins, called staterooms in those days.

Built by Egyptian shipwrights at Alexandria in 1933 to a very high standard, *Ionia* proved so well balanced that the owner declared he could steer her with one hand without needing any tiller lines in any moderate breeze, which for a yacht of 29 tons TM was highly gratifying. Like Henry Howard's *Alice*, which she resembled in many characteristics, *Ionia* showed her ability as a safe offshore seaboat when, a year later, she rode out a severe northerly gale (probably like the one that wrecked the Roman merchant ship of St Paul) riding ahull under bare poles with the board lowered only a foot or two. In a letter the owner described her as 'lying like a duck, swept by fine spray but shipping no solid water', and with an easy glide to her motion before the seas. Although I had a brief opportunity to see her hauled out in the REYC shed in 1941 when on Naval duties in Alexandria, I never had an opportunity to sail in *Ionia*, and her owner sadly died soon after the end of the war.

While production of the magazine with a minimum staff generally filled the days, I managed to put together another book, this time a collection of what I termed cameos of cruising, just reflections on aspects of sailing in the waters of the Thames Estuary and the Essex and Suffolk coasts. It was published by Edward Arnold in 1932 under the title *The Magic of the Swatchways*, and it so caught the fancy of like minded readers that it has gone into a number of editions, both hard- and softback, has been described even as a yachting classic, and is still selling today. Meanwhile, I had to find time at night and at weekends every so often to meet new orders for yacht designs. It was at times immensely gratifying and absorbing, but weekend sailing just had to go by the board!

For the budding naval architect learning how to work out a complete set of lines and plans for a new design to be built is like learning the rudiments of handling a boat under sail: the inspiration does not always come easily, and the work demands a great deal of concentration, patience, a good eye for fair and flowing lines, a steady draughtsman's hand and, perhaps above all, 'an eye for a boat'. Articles in the yachting press and text books for the aspiring designer have never been prolific or even easy to find; although some technical colleges, like Southampton University, have offered courses in yacht designing in recent years.

Of books on the subject the reader might find the following titles of value if he can obtain a copy:

Elements of Yacht Design Norman L Skene, A & C Black, London
Design of Sailing Yachts Gutelle, Nautical Publishing Co, London
Yacht Designing and Planning H I Chapelle, International American Boatbuilding Society
Sailing Yacht Design D Philips-Birt, Adlard Coles, London
Basic Naval Architecture K C Barnaby, Hutchinson, London

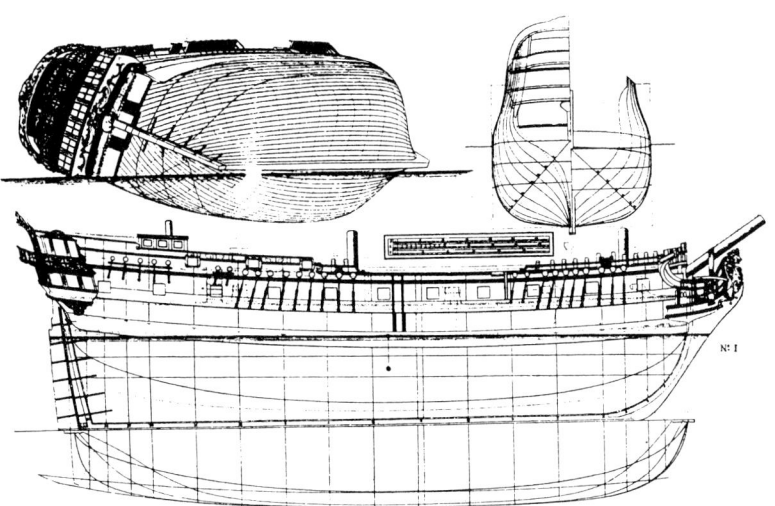

A beautiful example of the art of the eighteenth-century ship draughtsman. From a drawing by Frederik Chapman in 1768 of a small frigate's lines, and perspective view of her careened.

Much practical advice on seagoing yacht design will be found in *Offshore* by John Illingworth (Adlard Coles, 1963), while a useful series of articles, 'Yacht Design for Beginners', by F B R Brown, ARINA, appeared in *Yachting Monthly* issues of November, December 1960, January, February, April and May 1961.

What drawing instruments will be required as tools of the trade by the aspiring yacht architect could be a subject for debate. Elaborate and expensive instruments will not necessarily make an outstanding architect: it is indeed surprising what can be achieved with determination, an eye for a boat and the simplest drawing aids. For taking up the work seriously, however, with the intention of having yachts built to one's designs, the following list of tools is suggested as worth investing in sooner or later.

1. Large drawing board, say 60in × 30in, for 1 : 16 to 1 : 10 scale plans.
2. Second drawing board, say 36in by 27in, for sail plans and smaller work.
3. Three wood splines (battens) from 24in to 60in. More to be added when needed.
4. Six to eight lead spline weights, 2½lbs to 4lbs, with point or hook ends.
5. Assorted long sweep, and multiple curve, plastic curves.
6. T-squares of width to suit both drawing boards.
7. Set squares, triangles, one 30 × 60 degrees, one 45 × 90 degrees.
8. Steel, or edged plastic, straight edge, 12in and 24in suitable.
9. Architect's scale rule, marked for $\frac{1}{16}$in to 1in scales.

10 Compasses, 4in to 6in, with pen and pencil fitments and extension bars.
11 Pair of dividers, 4in to 8in.
12 A flexible curve, 12in or 18in, for short curves and bends.

Drawing materials would be covered by lead pencils (medium to hard H to 4H); ink pens, plain drawing and screw hatching; erasers (the rubber pencil type is useful for small erasions, not requiring a perforated metal erasing shield); good class tracing paper in rolls or separate sheets of width required.

Sooner or later a set of D K (Dixon Kemp) ship curves for hull sections and other short or reverse curves will be a valuable purchase. Where there is much work to be done in the drawing office professional naval architects rely on a planimeter for measuring the areas of oddly shaped figures. With its hinged arms and travelling wheel, its vernier and uncanny recording device, a planimeter could well be the most expensive of a yacht designer's instruments, and its purchase could be left to a later date, or dropped as a Christmas hint to an admiring aunt.

For measuring areas of a yacht's sections, waterlines, underwater profile and such oddly shaped figures I have worked happily with rigid sheets of clear plastic which have been ink-engraved with ¼in, ½in, ¾in and 1in squares. With the transparent sheet laid over the part to be measured, a careful count of the squares and portions of squares within the figure has been found, time and again, as accurate as a planimeter, and easier to handle. While to find the centre of, say, the yacht's underwater profile (centre of lateral resistance, or CLR) without a planimeter, a simple method is to trace the profile on a thin sheet, paste this lightly onto a level and rigid piece of cardboard, cut out round the tracing, and balance on a fine point. This CG of the figure will be the theoretical CLR of the yacht's underwater profile. The same practical method can be applied to body plan, sections and other shaped figures with sufficient accuracy in the finished design to dismay the most meticulous architects.

A fair amount of painstaking measuring and calculating is unavoidable if the finished yacht is to weigh anything like the estimates and float anywhere near the drawn waterline, and to stand up to the sail area planned for her. But these calculations cannot be bypassed and have to be worked out. For this reason the pocket calculator has proved a huge improvement over the old slide rule. It is the accumulation of these hull and stability calculations, added to the drafting of lines and construction plans, accommodation layout and deck plans, sail and rigging drawing and the drawing up of the yacht's specifications that adds all the hours to the designer's job and which some clients find difficult to understand.

Fredk. Shepherd, my mentor, always produced a shapely and well balanced yacht which was pleasing to the eye, and at the same time a thoroughly able boat at sea. In my work I have endeavoured to follow this principle, and have found there is much truth in the old saying, 'if a ship *looks* right, she'll *be* right'. I have never been tempted to try my hand at racing yachts with all the parameters and complications of the rating rules. My aim from the very first has been a good looking cruising boat which not only offers comfort below decks for the owner and friends, but has also a sturdy hull and gear which can face up to whatever weather conditions are to be expected sooner or later at sea, without the fear that she might break up or capsize and founder.

If the plans for a really shallow draft boat — by which I mean with a draft less than 40 per cent of the beam — are on the board, an essential requirement for my own satisfaction has been for her to be given sufficient ballast weight on her keel to enable her to be self-righting should she ever be laid flat by a knockdown, or rolled over by a sea breaking all over her. The subject of what is meant by the term 'a good seaboat' is far from exact and therefore difficult to define, but I think most seamen and sailing types who are familiar with bad weather conditions at sea will recognise what constitutes a seaworthy vessel and what does not.

What ingredients in a design go to make a seaworthy yacht, and how in recent years the grotesque ultra-lightweight hulls which have been introduced under the International Offshore Rules have influenced the design of contemporary so-called family cruising boats, has been logically examined in a recent book, *Seaworthiness: The Forgotten Factor* by C A Marchaj, published by Adlard Coles in 1986.

This is a major work on a subject which has needed clarifying for some time, for the varying behaviour in storm weather of different types of yachts, from the traditional long keel cruising boats of the prewar period through the trends of the 1960s and 1970s to the rule cheaters of today, has not been fully understood hitherto. For the emerging yacht designer who aims to produce either rule cheaters or cruising boats, Marchaj's book can be described with confidence as recommended reading.

III

From the time that the word *yacht* was first introduced into the English language, when Charles II at the Reformation in 1660 was presented by the Dutch with a state *jacht* called *Mary*, sailing matches between pleasure vessels rapidly became the sport of kings and noblemen on the lower Thames. And since speed of sailing was demanded by their sporting owners, the builders of these highly decorated vessels naturally copied the lines of the fastest small vessels of the day, and so yachts began to resemble the Revenue cutters with their enormous sail plans.

Sailing clubs came into being to organise sailing matches between members as well as fleet manoeuvres. Amongst the earliest of these institutions were the Royal Cork Yacht Club founded in 1720, the Royal Thames (begun as the Cumberland Fleet) in 1775, and the Royal Yacht Squadron in 1815 which were followed by sailing clubs throughout the world where sailing for pleasure could be carried out. Gradually, the yachts themselves adopted a pattern which showed the cutters with bluff bows and straight stems and the schooners with clipper, or fiddlehead bows, both having long, square counters — no gentlemen's yacht in the last century would be seen with a humble transom stern.

The old full bows with a fine run aft to the stern — the so-called cod's-head-mackerel-

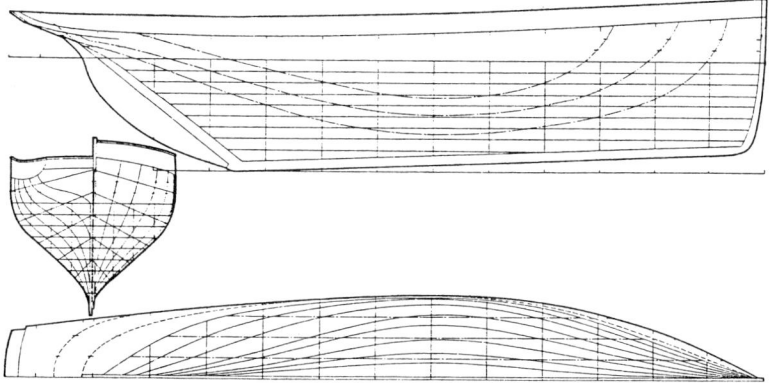

Lines of the 68-foot cutter Volante *built by Harvey at Wivenhoe in 1851, showing the peg top midsection and the hollow bow lines.*

tail type — began to be superceded by yachts with a fine, often hollow, entrance and a shorter keel, which was achieved by giving the stern post a great rake. The accompanying lines of the cutter *Volante*, designed and built by John Harvey at Wivenhoe, Essex, in 1851 clearly illustrate this type. With her pegtop shape of midsection *Volante* was 68 feet 4 inches overall, 61 feet 6 inches on the waterline with 14 feet 9 inches beam and 10 feet draft. She was one of the yachts that competed with the schooner *America*, which was almost twice the cutter's size.

One effect that the Thames Measurement rating rule began to have on the design of yachts was due to the penalty it levied on a yacht's beam. The next generation of

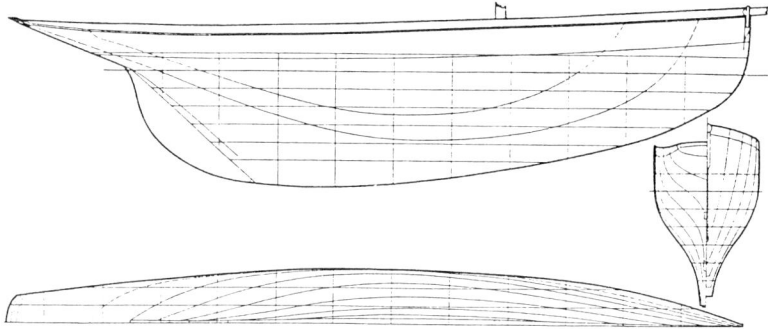

The effect of contemporary rating rules on a yacht's beam is seen in the 'plank on edge' hull of the 63-foot cutter Clara *built by Will Fife II in 1884. With a WL length of 53 feet her beam was only 9.2 feet with a 9.8 feet draft.*

designers who were appearing on the scene realised how they could take advantage of the loopholes the rule allowed by introducing yachts which became progressively narrower so as to gain a lower rating. The dodges of the racing boys in cheating the latest rules have been going on for more than a hundred years, and they have not finished with them yet!

To enable these narrow beamed yachts to carry their very large sail plans, more and more ballast had to be stowed below. At first all the lead was inside but then tentatively part of the ballast was attached to the bottom of the wood keel where its weight was more effective. This ratio of weight on keel to inside ballast was increased until all the lead ballast was hung on the bottom of the keel. These narrow gutted yachts with a great weight of lead on the keel became known as 'leadmines', and developed into a type of English yacht which was completely eschewed by American designers and builders with their preference for generous beam and moderate draft.

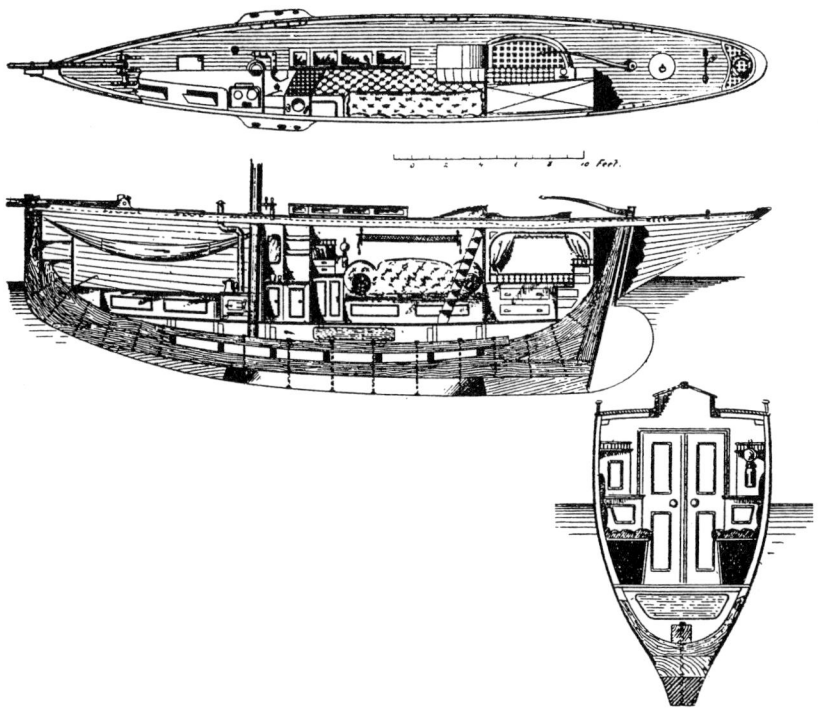

This interior plan of a typical small '6 beams to length' cutter of 1882, with 36 foot WL and 6 foot beam, shows why only thin men were welcome below. Like all contemporary 'plank on edge' yachts she would sail on her ear in anything above a moderate breeze, and drive her lean bows into any head seas.

At first the lead was attached to the underside of the wood keel by means of a row of flitch plates let in flush on both sides of the wood keel and lead with athwartship bolts. I recall that our own 6-ton cutter *Undine*'s lead keel was held on with these plates, which were a sure indication of the period in which she had been built; namely in 1873. The accompanying lines of the cutter *Clara*, designed and built by Will Fife Junior in 1884, show a typical leadmine type yacht with the effect of the rating rule since the building of the Harvey *Volante*. With length overall of 63 feet 4 inches *Clara* was 52 feet 9 inches on the waterline with a beam of 8 feet 4 inches and a draft 9 feet 8 inches. With 37 tons displacement her sail area was 3221 square feet.

This plank-on-edge type with its very fine lines forward and aft had its many supporters amongst the racing fleets, for in the sheltered waters of the Clyde and the Solent these yachts could show their paces against the older, fuller bowed vessels. They could slice their way through a short chop but in any fresh to strong breeze these narrow yachts 'sailed on their ear' (40 to 50 degrees heel with lee deck buried was usual) and in any head sea they were extremely wet and at times a danger to any hands on deck.

Down below, the accommodation in a six-beams-to-length cutter was as cramped as might be expected. This is clearly seen in the accompanying interior drawing of a typical boat of this type. This plank on edge cutter measured 42 feet 6 inches on deck, 36 feet waterline, with 6 feet beam and 6 feet 6 inches draft. Ballast on the keel was 5 tons with 3 tons of lead inside. One cannot help wincing at the thought of what would happen to a yacht of this design which has run aground on the sands (it *has* been known) on the ebb and awaits the next tide to float her off — if it would before filling her.

In an attempt to encourage a less extreme type of boat the Yacht Racing Assocation in 1882 adopted a new rating rule which had been proposed by Dixon Kemp, the yacht designer, when he was editor of *The Field*. Expressed as $\frac{(L + B)^2 \times B}{1730}$ it became known as the 1730 Rule, but once again it penalised the yacht's beam measurement and in the hands of the new generation of yacht designers it opened the door to even more extreme attempts to cheat the rule.

The ultimate in this plank-on-edge conception was reached in 1886 when a twenty-five-year old designer, William Evans Paton, went all out to beat the rule with a new 5-tonner. He built the famous *Oona* which measured 46 feet on deck, 34 feet on the waterline with only 5 feet 6 inches beam but a draft of 8 feet. On a total sailing displacement of 12.5 tons her lead keel weighed no less than 9.6 tons, achieving a record ballast ratio of 76.8 per cent.

Paton employed his own form of light construction with double skin mahogany planking on lightweight steel frames, and the stresses on every part of the hull were calculated in greater detail than had so far been applied to small yachts. The planning of this boat was far ahead of its time, and it is recorded that the designer paid daily visits to the yard to supervise every detail of the construction.

In May 1886, *Oona* sailed on her maiden voyage from Southampton for the Clyde with her owner and designer, a professional skipper and two hands on board. On passage to Kingston (now Dun Laoghaire), her first port of call, she delighted all on board with her obvious ability to sail fast, although showing all the heeling and nose diving characteristics of her type. After leaving next day she encountered a severe easterly gale which embayed her off Malahide. No one knows exactly what happened next, but the light hull was driven ashore minus its keel and smashed up on the rocks, while all on board lost their lives. The lead keel was never located, and it is probable that it tore itself clear of its fastenings while still in deep water as the little vessel tried desperately to claw off the lee shore.

The tragic end of the ingeniously conceived *Oona* put a dampener on the leadmine type which, added to successive defeats of the challenging English cutters by the Yankee centreboarders in the America's Cup contests, induced the Yacht Racing Association the same year to adopt what became known as the length and sail area rule (and expressed as $\frac{L \times SA}{6000}$, using length on load waterline) in the belief that this would produce a better class of yacht. It was not long, however, before these irrepressible yacht designers scented loopholes in even this simple formula and introduced the so-called spoon bow with flattened U sections. They also carried similar sections aft in a long counter, resulting in a greatly increased waterline length when heeled.

Needless to say, owners demanded similar lines for their new yachts, whether they intended to race them or merely cruise, and towards the end of the century spoon bows and long flat counters with ever shorter keels became the fashion. The effect of this rule in an out and out racer is clearly shown in the accompanying lines of a large steel racing cutter designed in 1898. It will be seen how the very flat U sections in the long bow, which are carried right down to the fore end of the keel, are repeated in the sections of the long flat counter, and how in the plan view the ends of the waterlines are snubbed in towards the centreline at both ends of the hull, like the underside of a tablespoon.

Owners who followed this fashion so that their yachts would at least 'look like the racing fleet' soon learnt the defects of the type. Closehauled in anything of a chop they would pound heavily, shaking the mast and rigging and sending showers of spray aft, giving the owner and his guests a rough ride even in moderate conditions. In something of a head sea, conditions aboard, especially in the fo'c'sle, were often intolerable and opened seams became a danger. When lying at anchor in a weather going tide the flat counter slammed and shook the yacht in much the same way, reminding the owner of his unwise choice of a boat. Amongst cruising yachts this fashion did not last long — only a decade or so — and more healthy designs began to appear, while for the racing fraternity a new rule was introduced with yet more hopes for a sensibly designed racing fleet.

This is not the place, however, to examine the development of the rating rules and their effect on design, for this book is devoted more to the designs of cruising yachts. Let it suffice that the rating rules, and especially the International Offshore Rule, have steadily become more intricate right up to the present day, and they will doubtless continue to

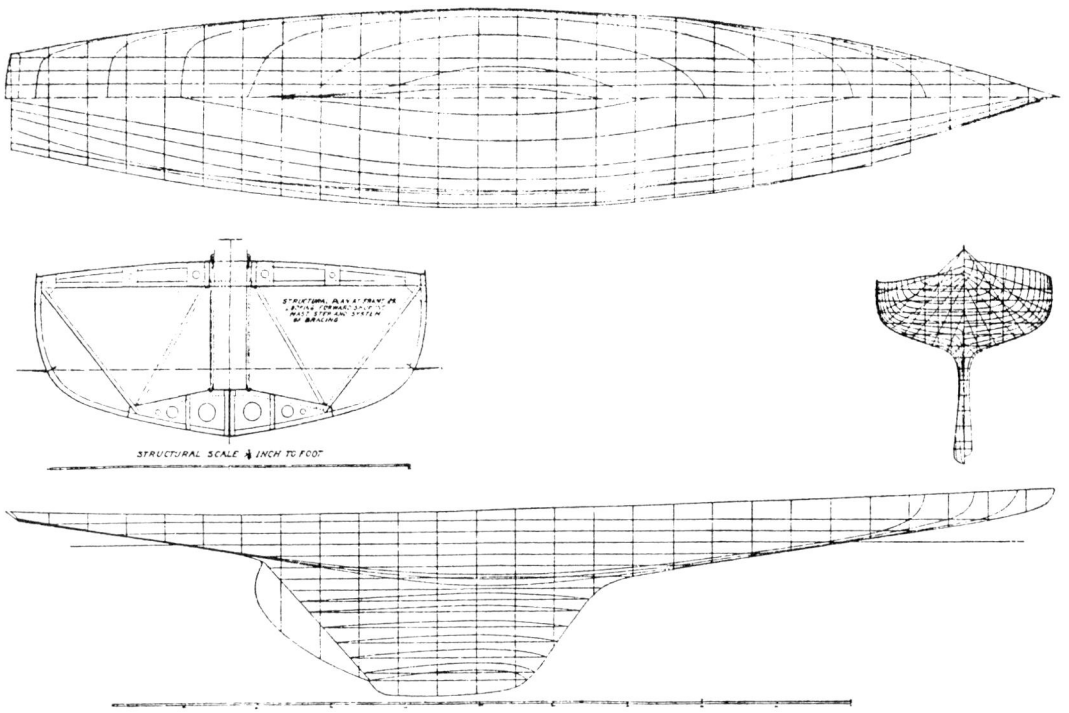

Rating rules at it again! An extreme type of spoon bow and flat counter stern racer built of steel in 1898. For a time, yachtsmen tended to copy this type so as to be in the fashion, but the effects of the flat bow and stern sections made life uncomfortable on board except in anything other than a calm.

do so for many years to come. The student who seeks to pursue the subject will find it discussed in books on yacht racing and in those sections of the yachting press which are given to racing matters.

The notion of cruising in small boats as distinct from match sailing had its beginnings about the middle of the Victorian era with groups of what were called Corinthian yachtsmen who followed their own way of life in a variety of small craft which were not even intended for racing. Although it is on record that the Atlantic was first crossed in a small sailing boat in 1866 (by two Americans, William Hudson and Frank Fitch, who sailed their three-masted 26-foot iron lifeboat *Red White and Blue* from east to west in 36 days), the pioneer of the small sailing cruiser in this country is generally acknowledged to have been John MacGregor, who published his book *Voyage Alone in the Yawl Rob Roy* in 1867.

The appearance of this charmingly written chronicle appears to have fired the imagination of a Lieutenant E Middleton, an irrascible eccentric, who promptly had a 3-ton yawl likewise built by *Rob Roy*'s builders, Forrestt of Limehouse. In this boat Middleton made a singlehanded voyage westabout round England in 1869. *The Cruise of the Kate* was published soon after (with a second edition in 1888) and illustrated with spirited engravings, and despite the author's heroic style (he was an authority on Virgil) this quaint book clearly shows some of the difficulties the pioneer singlehanders had in cruising along unknown and sparsely buoyed coasts at that time.

Of all the books which had influence on future generations of cruising yachtsmen from the 1870s onwards, the palm is usually accorded to R T McMullen and his classic book *Down Channel*, which has since appeared in various editions. His exploits in his various yachts showed what one man with determination could achieve on his own. For the student collector of old yacht cruising books there have been others which are still a delight to read, for example:

Cruises in Small Yachts and Big Canoes H Fiennes Speed (1883)
Falcon on the Baltic E F Knight (1890)
Sailing Tours, Vols 1-5 Frank Cowper (1892-96)
Swale, Swin and Swatchways H L Jones (1892)
Sailing Alone Around the World Captain Joshua Slocum (1898)
Vagaries of Lady Harvey Frank Cowper (1930)
Venturesome Voyages Captain Voss (1913)

As the numbers of like minded cruising sailing men began to increase, so groups founded new clubs devoted to their version of the sport. The Corinthian Yacht Club was formed in 1872 with its small clubhouse on the Isle of Grain at the mouth of the Medway, and at first its members mostly made cruises in company in the Thames Estuary, like smaller units of the Cumberland Fleet of a century before. Later, the club moved to new headquarters at Burnham-on-Crouch, where it became the Royal Corinthian and a leading racing centre. Another group, founded in 1880, later became the Royal Cruising Club, and within three years owners of a north country type of small centreboard yawl launched the Humber Yawl Club, and encouraged a distinctive type of spartan cruiser. By 1887, the Waterwags, a lively class of boats and owners in Dublin Bay, offered between races an Irish version of the small boat camping-cruising syndrome, and this aspect of sailing just for pleasure with eating and sleeping facilities at hand was well on its way to become an important part of the yachting scene. By the turn of the century boatyards throughout the country were building sound little ships with comfort below decks as a major conception of their design.

Following a visit to the United States, where I had the opportunity to meet and talk with a number of owners, designers and builders with whom I had been in correspondence, I was able to produce a book discussing the abilities of well designed yachts of shallow draft for blue water cruising as well as for inshore sailing. *Little Ships and Shoal Waters* appeared in 1937 with a selected number of shallow draft designs by British, American and Continental yacht designers with their comments. In line with the traditional methods of timber construction of the period there were also included designer's specifications and a specimen builders' agreement for the construction of a typical 36-foot yawl with the yard methods described. During the London blitz in 1940 all the printers' type and plates for this book, among others, were destroyed; but with the introduction of new photoprinting techniques developed later, fresh editions have been issued more recently by Conway Maritime Press.

As a result of the notes I had made during my visit to America I started to draft preliminary plans for my next boat, with a sturdy centreboarder in mind. From the beginning I found the lines were following closely those of the powerful, broadbeamed cutter *Scoter*, which had so captivated my imagination in my presailing days as she swung to the tide in the Bight at Ipswich 20 years before. As the drawings took shape on the board, my boat, *Lone Gull*, sported the same curved stem, transom stern, shallow hull and deep bulwarks around the deck; she was to be 28.5 feet on deck with 10 feet beam and a draft of just over 3 feet with iron ballast keel and the board raised.

When I showed my plans to Len Johnson, of Johnson and Jago, Leigh-on-Sea, and asked him to build her for me he remarked 'Why, she's just like a little *Scoter*!' The yard hands knew the old *Scoter* well, for she had spent several winters at the yard when owned by the marine artist Colin Grierson. While similar in outward characteristics, my boat, however, did not copy the 14-tonner's enormous ¾ inch steel centreplate with its mangle wheel assisted lifting gear; *Lone Gull* followed Yankee practice with her L-shaped centreboard built up with 2-inch oak planks, which was to prove so easy to work that it could be lowered and raised by hand without need of the three-part purchase. *Scoter*, however, had given me my first ideas about a well proportioned centreboard boat and thus influenced my new boat, building at Leigh in 1938. I was not to know, then, that many years later I was to be asked to design an updated version of the old *Scoter*, 34 feet by 11 feet beam, by a yachtsman who then owned a narrow gutted, deep draft Scandinavian racing boat and had sailed in company with his friend's broad centreboarder, and fallen for her. The result, *Idle Duck*, is described later in this book.

Lone Gull turned out all I had hoped of her; never pulling hard on the helm, sailing at only ten degrees or so, and dipping her scuppers only when hard pressed in breezy weather. Not a racer, but a sweet tempered old girl with a liking for wriggling up narrow creeks and anchoring for the night where few other yachts cared to venture. That might not be so these days, when there are now so many light draft twin keelers and drop-keel dishes who enjoy swarming together wherever there is water to float them!

The centreboard arrangement intrigued many visitors aboard, as the fore end was beneath the cabin sole while the after part of the board rose inside the case which extended to the cabin roof, where it formed a convenient fore and aft bulkhead for the snug galley to port. Johnson and Jago built three near-sisters to the plans, but with keels deepened 9 inches and centreboard omitted. One of them, a gaff cutter rigged to order, went out to the West Indies where she fulfilled a charter service for many years.

September 1939 came, and with the country at war *Lone Gull*, in common with all pleasure craft, spent the next six years laid up at her builders' yard, happily only splattered with Leigh mud from one or two near-misses in bombing raids.

IV

Back in the London office after being demobilised, problems of austerity, paper shortages and rapidly rising costs had to be grappled with while many of us tried once more to fit into a daily commuter's life. The whole country seemed to be in a state of unrest, and the relief of being no longer at war and now able to enjoy the lights at night was tempered with a disillusion at the continuation of ration cards and shortages of everything.

Disputes which had never arisen in the war years began to come to the surface, and in its small way the *Yachting Monthly* which had had an unbroken run since its launch in 1906, and had not missed a single issue throughout two world wars, now found itself caught up in industrial strikes and unable to produce issues of the magazine. It seemed a sad state of business at the time, but only a forerunner of the industrial troubles that were to come.

The yachting scene was also slow to pick up after the war ended. Many boats which had been left under covers in mud berths, or hauled out at yards in the open, suffered where the ravages of six years of wet weather and sunshine had managed to get at them. The effects of rainwater in the bilge or lodged in pools against deck fittings and lockers had in many cases brought on such extensive areas of wood rot that some of the older boats were beyond repair, and never sailed again. In many cases their owners could never be traced, enveloped somewhere perhaps in the war.

Enemy action had destroyed sails and gear stored in yard sheds, and their replacement was a problem as canvas for new sails and covers, and timber for boat repairs could not yet be released. For a year or two everything in the yachting business was at a standstill, and special permits had to be obtained to carry out any repair work, while new building of pleasure craft was prohibited. Timber of all grades was in desperately short supply and urgently needed for the repair of bombed buildings and for the new housing schemes.

Gradually, as the 1940s drew to a close the position began to ease, and yachtsmen took every desperate way they could find to get another boat — even to building it in the back garden. One good innovation which had come out of the war was a truly waterproof glue which could make plywood impervious to wet conditions. Hitherto, ordinary plywood could not face outside weather conditions without delaminating, and was therefore useless for boats. So *marine ply* had been born, and amateur as well as professional boatbuilders learnt how to construct hulls with flat sides and V-bottoms joined by chines. They were easy to build without skilled shipwright labour, and promised to be really weather resistant.

Thus was opened up a new era of deadrise or chine boat building, which enabled the home handiman to construct the boat of his dreams within a few steps of his kitchen door. The yachting press began to offer their readers sets of simple plans for home building of a variety of small sailing and power craft. In the *Yachting Monthly* we introduced plans for a simple 13-foot 6-inch *Junior* day boat, which was followed by a 16-foot *Senior* of the same model with a two berth cabin, both designed specially by Kenneth M Gibbs. Some hundreds of these two pioneer build-yourself designs were to be completed during the next decade.

Readers' demand for something a little bigger with more accommoation resulted in our issuing plans for the 19-foot single chine *Wild Duck* and the 20-foot round bilge 3-Tonner with a three berth cabin, both to design by Alan H Buchanan.

About this time the fitting of small yachts with deep bilge keels or fins was introduced in only a tentative way, for the demand for moorings, even those that dried out, had not yet become so acute. This fitting of what amounted to three keels was not an entirely new idea, for previous attempts had been tried but had not been generally accepted by the conservative yachting community. For instance, as far back as 1890 a consortium of Irish yachtsmen calling themselves 'The Graphics' had a 60-foot ketch yacht specially designed and built for them for exploring all the shallow bays and inlets on the coast between Dundalk and Waterford. The party included members interested in ornithology, painting and sketching, the law, photography, medicine and music, and all could play an instrument so as to make up an extemporare orchestra on board. The yacht, *Iris*, had a 12-foot 6-inch beam and a draft restricted to only 3 feet 6 inches so as to settle on the foreshore by having two stout bilge keels in addition to the main central lead ballast keel: in short, three keels in all.

For her purpose *Iris* was described as a great success, proving a handy ship with an unexpectedly easy motion in bad weather, and able to fetch to windward much better than her owners and some of the local wiseacres had expected. In crowded anchorages she was able to escape in storm weather from the dragging anchors of the big fishermen and other yachts, while on still evenings when she was sitting close inshore along some bay on her keels the strains of laughter and an orchestra rising from her skylights doubtless often puzzled or enchanted the locals. The accompanying sketch, taken from a

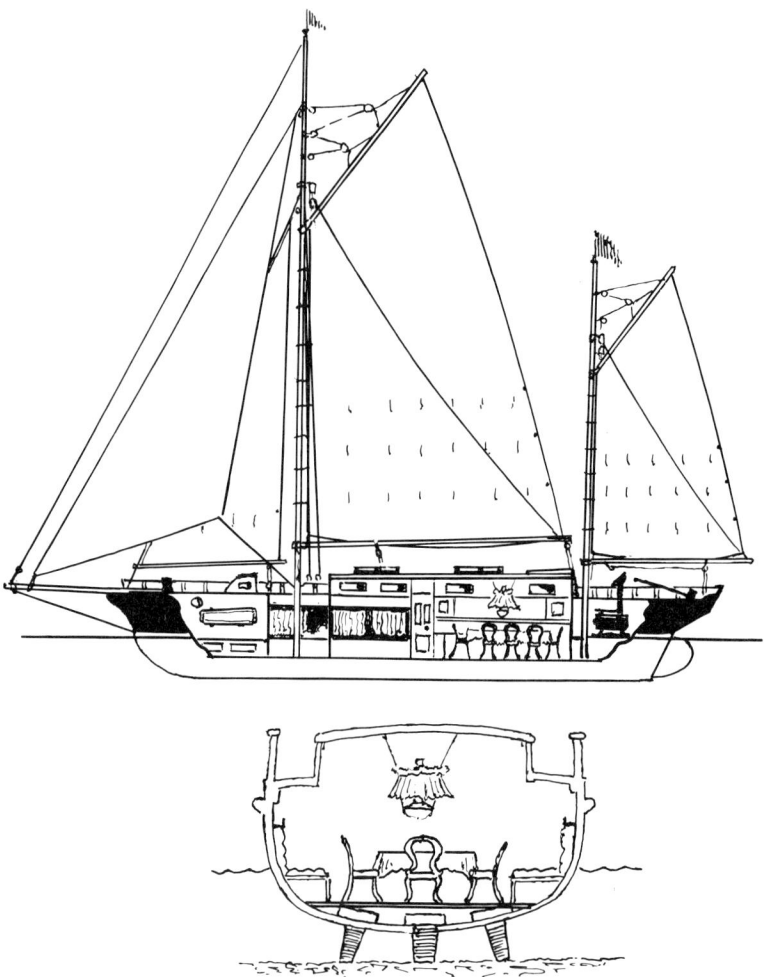

An early pioneer? The 60-foot ketch Iris *with three keels was built in 1890 for an Irish syndicate.*

contemporary diagram, shows her shallow draft and her sturdy construction, and the comfortable saloon where the Graphics hung their paintings and shoreline specimens. But *Iris* with all her useful qualitites for the peace loving cruising party was only a one-off and not repeated. She was too far ahead of her time.

It was the Hon R A Balfour (now Lord Riverdale) who next opened up the investigation into twin keels when he designed and built the 24-foot *Bluebird* in 1928. This little sloop had a number of innovative features which included twin rudders in line with the two keels and a bipod lowering mast. In her Balfour cruised widely around the north of Scotland, and she was eventually replaced by a greatly enlarged version in *Bluebird of Thorne*, a 48-footer with twin keels and rudders which the owner designed in collaboration with Arthur Robb and had constructed of steel in 1939. This interesting little ship, I am told, eventually sailed out to New Zealand. Meanwhile, Robert Clark designed a 25-feet gunter sloop, *Buttercup*, with a torpedo shaped hull of double-skin mahogany and twin keels, which was built at the Rowhedge Ironworks on the river Colne in 1937, and proved her qualities not only on the shore but in a number of long offshore cruises.

It was not until the great upsurge of yachting took place in the 1950s and mooring space became an increasing problem that the combination of shallow draft and bilge keels to enable a boat to squat upright at low water that this type of boat became accepted. The pioneer producer of the miniature cabin boat with twin bilge keels was undoubtedly Robert Tucker, who introduced his 17½-foot, two-berth chine sloop, *Silhouette* class, intended for home construction with marine ply. These cleverly conceived little cruisers were to be built in many hundreds over the years, updated in GRP form as the *Silhouette* Mk II, to become probably the most numerous class of small cabin boat to date.

Home boat building, which had long been common enough in Australia and New

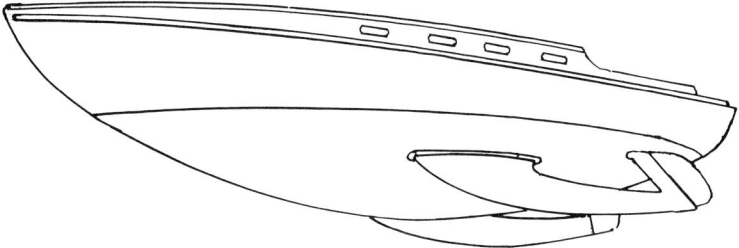

Perspective view of Lord Riverdale's advanced design of 48-foot twin keel and rudder profile on Bluebird of Thorne.

Zealand, Canada and South Africa where few yards existed that could build a yacht to order, suddenly became an industry of its own in Britain, and it started a growing demand for suitable building plans. On the *Yachting Monthly* we launched plans of the 24-foot *Eventide* chine sloop with central iron ballast keel and twin bilge keel plates for marine ply construction, and following readers' demands a 26-foot version was made available. Plans for a single-chine 30-footer, the *Waterwitch*, next appeared and offered alternative versions with either bilge keels and 3 foot draft, or a Mk II barge type with 2 foot draft and leeboards. These designs became popular with owner-builders, and the total of all four types built and sailing in most parts of the world eventually ran into over two thousand, with the Eventide Owners' Association supplying plans and an advice service.

What gave yachting the greatest upsurge, and in fact revolutionised the industry, was the introduction of the resin glass reinforced plastic method of moulding which was introduced in the early 1950s. Long before the Hitler war we had been receiving readers' letters with much the same idea of mass production of yachts. A typical letter read:

SIR — Instead of building yachts as we have been doing for more than a hundred years, shaping by skilled craftsmen hundreds of pieces of wood to be fitted together with hundreds more screws, copper nails, rivets and bolts, with all those carefully fitted joints which are liable to leaks and eventual rot, would it not be possible for our Plastics Industry (say, ICI?) to produce a plastic mix which could be poured into a mould, and when set and hardened would result in a complete yacht's hull of an approved design? Any number of identical hulls could be run off from the same moulds. Just think what the saving in the cost of each boat would be! — Hopeful, Hamble, Hants.

But the plastics industry was not quite ready for this miracle, and yachtsmen had to wait until some years after the war for this revolution to take place. When it came it was not quite as simple as pouring into a hollow mould, but identical hulls could be produced in moulds by the glass fibres and polyester mix being laid up by hand without the need for shipwright or any other acquired skills. In its way this new production method was a miracle and seemed to be the answer to the yachtsman's prayer, and as demand for new pleasure craft of all kinds escalated, many of the old established boatyards turned their men over to completing hulls as they were delivered from the moulding companies.

The demand also attracted large numbers of newcomers to boatbuilding, like firms which had been making plastic domestic appliances, baths, washbasins, radio and television cabinets and the like. Jumping on the bandwagon with pound signs in their eyes, some of these manufacturers introduced sorry specimens of ill-conceived boats, and the GRP yacht at first earned a bad name. And the traditional yachtsman, did *he* welcome the answer to his long awaited prayer for inexpensively moulded yachts? Alas, his reaction, at least at first, could be expressed as: 'I don't like it! The stuff doesn't *look* right in a boat, and it doesn't *smell* right, and it's difficult to attach fittings to it. It'll crumble away in sunlight, and if the boat hits anything underway, it'll split open like an eggshell. Give me the sight and feel and smell of good wood every time. You can keep your plastic soap dishes!'

Despite the early prejudices, which took many forms, production of resinglass yachts and power boats soon extended to all countries throughout the world where pleasure craft were built, and a revolution in quantity production of boats could now take place. Through successive boat shows in London from 1954 onwards and later in many other countries, the early inexperienced manufacturers folded up (to return to their plastic bowls and radio cabinets) and left the industry free to produce the fine extensive range of ever larger yachts and motor cruisers which have made yachting what it is today.

Boating for pleasure in all its forms has become worldwide the greatest leisure industry, made possible by the increase in peoples' earning power, greater leisure time and longer holidays, and enormously improved facilities for boating in yacht harbours and marinas and general marine services. That this has resulted in the waters in the more popular areas becoming grossly overcrowded is not to be denied; indeed, rivers and creeks, inland waterways, the Norfolk Broads, lakes and reservoirs where sailing and power boating can be enjoyed are already congested, and boating space is at a premium.

The extent of this explosion in pleasure boating in recent years can be gauged from a comparison with pre-war conditions. In 1939 it is recorded that in the United Kingdom there were about 16,000 cruising and racing yachts, motor yachts and cruisers, speedboats, one-design sailing boats and class racing dinghies, but excluding rowing dinghies and outboard-powered boats. In 1986 the total of similar categories of pleasure craft in the UK was assessed at 380,000 boats, representing roughly a 23.75 fold increase. Bearing in mind the area of waters suitable for pleasure boating throughout the country has hardly increased at all, the demand for boating space is aggravated still more by the huge numbers of sailboards (or windsurfers) not included in the above figure. And all this has been made possible by the introduction of quantity produced hulls of all types in GRP from about 1950 onwards.

Today's designers and builders have available to them an almost bewildering choice of methods of constructing a yacht's hull, each with its own set of advantages and inevitable drawbacks. Apart from the traditional wood carvel and clinker (or lapstrake) construction, with or without the wood epoxy saturated technique (WEST) preservation against rot and decay, or the somewhat less skilled labour intensive marineply hull planking, any one of the following methods of building a small to medium size yacht can be followed:

— Strip planking, glued and edge-nailed on cross frames or fore and aft stringers.
— Double skin planking, inside diagonal, outside fore and aft on cross frames or stringers.
— Multi wood laminates, stapled and glued to light frames or stringers (known as the cold moulded process).
— Resinglass coated polyester foam sandwich.

- C-Flex fibreglass sheeting, covering a light hull framework of multi stringers or frames.
- Ferrocement, for hulls say 9 metres (28 feet) or over, offering a number of alternative methods of internal framing, using pipes, rodding, bow frames together with a variety of wire mesh.
- Steel, with single or multi chines, or with plate bending facilities and techniques for a round bilge hull.
- Aluminium alloy, employing similar techniques to steel building.

For sailing and power yachts of about 10 metres (33 feet) and over in length steel has much to recommend it for its great strength and its watertightness both on deck and below. The old bogey of constant corrosion and rust has been largely eliminated by modern methods of hull treatment during construction, and care taken in insulating all fittings of non-ferrous metals (brass, copper, bronze) from direct contact with the hull plating.

Given normal skills in welding techniques for working in steel, the home builder can find a steel hull a far simpler proposition than constructing a similar yacht in timber, providing he has chosen a straightforward design with single or multichines. A round bilge hull in steel is a different proposition, however, and necessitates the considerable skills of a plate bender with his heavy bending machine.

Aluminium alloy does appear to be the most desirable material for a small yacht, because it offers almost the same strength as steel together with its absence of leaks from above and below the waterline, and above all its light weight. In a small sailing yacht this last is a highly welcome factor, leading to either a lighter displacement overall and a better sailing performance, or for some requirements a higher ballast ratio. In this imperfect world there are always attendant snags in everything, and those in building in light alloy are: (a) the special techniques required in welding aluminium, (b) the care required to insulate this material from any other metal, and (c) the high cost of light alloy.

In time to come the costs of producing aluminium in quantity will doubtless be brought down by modern processes (as indeed were the high costs of steel reduced dramatically by new production processes introduced in the 1860s), but until that happens light alloy hulls will remain largely an ideal for the yachtsman with a comfortably deep purse.

Yacht designs have developed at an increasing rate in the past decade or so, and what was thought of as the last word in well planned cruising yachts in 1970 will look old fashioned in the eyes of many today. Apart from improved accommodation layouts, designs of galleys and the use of space below decks, and ideas for greater comfort and protection from the elements in the cockpit, strides have been made in the design of deck gear and sail handling.

From the old wooden roller foresail for small boats, and its successor the Wykeham Martin jib furling gear, which have both served sailing men since the turn of the century, the recent developments in roller furling and reefing headsail gears have introduced a new aspect to short-handed and solo sailing. Slab reefing with its ingenious use of pulleys and lines has taken much of the labour out of tucking reefs in a yacht's mainsail, while the furling mainsail which rolls itself into a wide slot on the after side of the hollow mast has come as an alternative to the well tried roller reefing main boom. Today's cruising yacht is made lighter and easier to manage by a small crew or singlehander than a boat half her tonnage 30 years ago.

Ingenious though many of these recent inventions are for making sailing easy work, yet few of them are entirely free of snags, the odd gremlin following sod's law, which can cause consternation.

For instance, it is an unhappy moment for the skipper when the expensive gear on the big jib won't roll up in a rising gale, the furling line parts with a bang, or through metal fatigue aloft the whole contraption collapses with its halyard over the bow. Or perhaps on a breezy occasion the neat self-furling mainsail refuses to fold away into the mast slot, like a reluctant stallion jibbing at entering its horsebox. These are all the kinds of things sailing men have had to grapple with for centuries, but now in more sophisticated, costly forms than ever before.

The sport of yachting in all its many forms has grown into a highly technical and complicated business. Modern technology has introduced countless labour saving devices for handling a boat, while synthetic materials for sails and running gear and high tensile steel for standing rigging have taken much of the labour out of maintenance. Today's yachtsman with his modern boat is saved much of the regular care and attention his forebears had to give to their decks and sails, ropes and standing rigging, and in consequence he has more time to sail and enjoy the boating life with his family, while the dreaded *plop-plop* on his berth from a leaking deck is an experience almost unknown amongst today's yotties.

The convenience of keeping one's boat in a well organised yacht harbour, and the prevailing habit of cruising from one marina to another for each night does away with the age old chore of picking up a swinging mooring — if there is one vacant — or anchoring and attending to the riding light. Navigation for the small yacht skipper has been revolutionised in recent years, and no longer need he work assiduously with compass and chart, for if his little ship has Decca or Satnav aboard he can learn his position in the thickest fog within a few hundred yards at the touch of a button. The common leadline is no longer to be found aboard many well-equipped yachts, for the echo sounder will tell him the depth beneath his keel, and in many cases will give him a warning sound when that depth is shoaling. And if help in bad weather is needed, or the plight of another yacht is to be transmitted to the Coast Guard or to a nearby ship, the radio telephone can prove a life-saving link with the rest of the world.

All of which should make sailing a happy, carefree vocation as it saves the yacht skipper so many of the anxieties which were all part of small boat cruising in the past. But all these breath taking innovations are of full value provided electrical faults don't develop in the system, and everything goes dead. In the accounts of many cruises when the yacht has been caught out in very bad weather, rising perhaps to storm conditions, that is precisely what has happened on all too many occasions. Then the owner finds himself entirely dependent on his own resources, like any sailor in the past century. And if he's totally unprepared for such an emergency, then it may be his tragedy.

All these technological aids to navigation and safety at sea turn the average modern yacht into a highly complex and expensive machine. So alluring are the colourful advertisements in the yachting magazines, so persuasive the sleek salesmen at the many boat shows, and so irresistible is the array of radar, RT, Satnav and the rows of dials, lights and switches over the chart table, like an airliner's flight deck, that the new yachtsman is converted to technology before he has even paid his deposit.

It is all happily conducive to trade in a multi-million pound leisure industry which is steadily growing according to Parkinson's Law. Yachting, in fact, has come full circle since the early years of this century: it has once more become a sport mainly for the wealthy — and the competitive.

Modest cruises up and down a coast appear to have lost their savour amongst today's yachtsmen, whose ventures take them and their families ever farther afield. Sailing to the Azores and on to the West Indies has turned into a regular annual flow like flotsam coming down on the ebb; a cruise to the Baltic and back is commonplace; the cold waters of the Orkneys and Shetlands see more yachts than ever before; while blue nosed skippers and their spouses have begun to sail round the coast of Iceland and into the arctic waters along the white shores of Greenland. To be able to claim to have gone farthest first has become as desirable an accolade as the racer's string of winning flags at the end of the regatta.

On the other hand there are still some sailing men and women who look to their boat as a means to obtain peace and an escape from the stress and bustle of life ashore.

Their great joy may well be to have a jolly sail in sparkling conditions to some quiet anchorage in a river, or maybe towards the head of a deserted creek, and there find a solitude and a quietness which is all too rare these days on land and in the air.

Looking back on all those years since I first started sailing in our old *Undine* during that scorching summer of 1921, the most enduring recollections (apart from memories of fast passages round the coast when both wind and tide were one's friends, or nights at sea when a full moon glinted on every little wave cap and the yacht's wake was a writhing trail of phosphorescent light) are those of quiet, secluded anchorages. In those days there were hundreds to be discovered in rivers and creeks and amongst the sands between the Alde and the Medway, the water I knew best. But in the harbours and creeks and lakes of the Wight area between Poole and Chichester harbours, and in the rivers and inlets of the lovely coasts of Devon and Cornwall the sailing man in search of peace and solitude had just as many choices in days gone by.

It was not only on the south coast or the West Country or the Thames Estuary, however, that a man and his boat could find peace, for I recall an occasion on the West Coast of Scotland more than 50 years ago which still has haunting memories. I had joined two friends from Glasgow aboard their old fashioned yawl for a week's cruise. It was during a rare spell of anticyclonic weather with sunny, warm days and a flat calm after sunset. We had brought up for the night close in to the shore of a small island, the only vessel of any kind in sight. Unable to sleep, while my companions snored happily, I crept out into the cockpit and sat in silence taking in the scene.

The water of the loch was like a mirror and its surface faithfully reflected the great dome of stars that looked down from the heavens. There were towns and hamlets and farms not so very far away, yet they could have been a thousand miles for not a sound of civilisation broke the stillness of the night. There were as yet no new roads carrying the drone of traffic, nor busy airlines murmuring across the skies. It was as if God had said to the world 'Peace, be still', and the heavens and the waters and the creatures on the land had obeyed.

As I sat and wondered at the peace of it all the only sound that could be heard was the magic music of the little burn somewhere along the nearby shore, and when I crept back to a still warm berth it was the last murmur I could hear before I dropped off into sleep. It was a memory to cherish for many years to come, and to remind me why so many of us conjure up the minor things, the little gratifications we have enjoyed by just being aboard our little ships in the silence of the night.

V

Estimating how any new yacht is going to behave at sea is a fascinating but uncertain exercise. The fluid in which any vessel floats is in itself an untameable medium, and how it will act on the hull of any boat under all conditions is not entirely predictable. Hence the regular use of models in ship testing tanks before a ship is built.

Certain characteristics of a new yacht's hull and rig, however, can give an idea of how she is *likely* to perform in a seaway, even though this will be only guesswork tinged with hope. It can be understood, for instance, that while old fashioned plank-on-edge yachts (like Fife's *Clara*, page 20, or the six-beams-to-length cutter on page 21) with their fine lines and long deep keels might sail very fast indeed, yet they could make no rapid changes of course however much helm you used, and would take their time in stays when changing from one tack to another. With their knife-like bows and heavy displacement they would drive through rather than lift over a head sea with their decks streaming and their crews getting very wet. And having little initial stability in their wedge-shaped sections they would rely on the weight of lead on the keel, acting like a pendulum, to keep them from being laid flat in strong squalls. But even in a moderately fresh freeze, say Force 6, they would sail on their ear with the lee rail buried beneath a seething rush of water, and life on board at such an angle would be anything but comfortable.

With the introduction of the spoon bow and flat counter type in the 1890s (page 24) an entirely different form of behaviour could be expected. In place of the slicing motion of the narrow yacht the flat U-sectioned bow would give her crew a bumpy ride over any head sea, bashing and pounding, shaking herself from stem to stern and sending sheets of fine spray aft. The pounding of these spoon-bowed yachts could become so excessive that it is said that one owner, whenever his skipper put the yacht on a close fetch into a head sea, cautiously slipped his false teeth (upper and lower) into his reefer pocket.

Leaving aside such extreme types, the traditional cruising yacht with a bow that is neither too lean nor too bluff and with a firm turn to her bilge amidships can be expected to behave moderately on all points of sailing. Her weight, or displacement, will give her a comparatively comfortable motion in a seaway, and should conditions deteriorate with the wind increasing to Force 8 or more, she can be laid hove-to with staysail aback and the mainsail (reefed) eased a little; or even left to ride it out under bare poles, ahull. In these conditions a good yacht will take care of herself and her crew.

In recent years, unhappily, this well tried type of cruising yacht has been replaced by a new generation of craft which have copied many of the more undesirable characteristics of the class racing boats. Of exceedingly light weight, made possible through contemporary materials and methods of construction, their hulls reflect the influences of the designers' attempts to cheat the Rules and gain the lowest possible rating. With shallow dishlike midsections, the narrow snout of a bow spreads out to an enormous beam like a pregnant bulge aft of amidships, and rounds into fat quarters and a wide stern of one form or another — forward sloping transom, slipper form, or dished in sugarscoop style. A short deep fin keel and right aft a dagger type rudder mounted on the transom or hung on an inboard vertical spindle with or without any protective skeg can offer their own problems. In shape the whole machine can be said to resemble a squashed orange pip.

These contemporary class machines have admittedly succeeded in twisting the Rules and obtained a low rating, but a more unbalanced hull it would be difficult to devise. When the boat heels under sail the stern rises on its fat quarters while her lean snout bores into the sea like a ploughshare; this causes her to slew into the wind, needing quick action by the helmsman to stop her from broaching. Running before a fresh to strong breeze, this tendency to sheer wildly to port or starboard can become almost uncontrollable, and the sight of a group of class racers under spinnakers rolling and weaving down wind and broaching with mainsails flogging and the seas breaking against their weather bilges offers an all-too-common delight for the press photographers.

Whilst, as we have seen, the behaviour of a yacht depends largely on the underwater shape of her hull and the balance or otherwise, between her fore body and aft body (bow and stern), the way she is rigged also plays an important part. There must be a satisfactory relation between the combined drive of the sails — reduced in theory to a single point, the centre of effort (CE) — and the theoretical point about which the yacht pivots in the water, the centre of lateral resistance (CLR).

If, for instance, the designer has stepped the mast too far forward, its weight may make the yacht wet in a seaway, but the CE of the sail plan will also be too far forward in its relation to the CLR, and it may tend to press the bows to leeward when on a wind. The yacht will then need *lee* helm to keep her on course: an undesirable condition at any time, and a dangerous one if she is hit by a heavy squall. On the other hand, with the mast stepped too far aft, and the pressure of the mainsail overriding that of the headsail(s), the balance of this sail plan aft of the CLR will press her stern to leeward, causing her to gripe and call for strong *weather* helm to keep her from weathercocking into the wind. In severe cases of griping the yacht can get completely out of control, and many collisions in the racing fleets have occurred through a combination of these causes.

To aim at what he hopes will turn out to be a well balanced yacht the designer has to find the position of the CLR of the immersed part of the hull. He can do this either by a series of calculations (with or without a planimeter, *see Chapter II*), or more simply by tracing the yacht's underwater profile onto stiff card, and locating the point on which it balances. This is not an exact point of the CLR, for in practice the more the yacht heels under her sails the more the submerged part of her hull will present a very different shape to the sea; and the combined pressures of the lee bow wave, the quarter wave and the general turbulence of the wake causes the pressure at the (theoretical) CLR to dance backwards and forwards like an excited puppy. And to make it even less exacting, those sails on the sail plan are never nice and flat as on the drawing; with sheets started they take up various curves so that the actual CE moves about like a wandering minstrel.

To allow for all this — and let us face it, it is largely guesswork — it has been customary with most cruising yacht designs to give the CE of the sail plan a lead of between 5 and 10 per cent of the load waterline (LWL) forward of the estimated CLR, depending on the general fineness or fullness of the yacht's underwater lines. Nowadays, with the increasing use of computers in yacht designing and the instant corrections possible with word-processors, the up-to-date naval architect with the skill and the necessary equipment will have the answers on the screen, and a beautifully balanced design, while we old stagers are still resharpening our pencils!

I have often been asked why some yachts are so much stiffer than others in standing up to their sails, and whether any of them could ever capsize when under sail. The power to carry sail, in other words a yacht's stiffness or stability, depends on several factors. The principal ones are the weight of ballast carried (inside or on the keel), and the shape of the hull amidships with either narrow beam, a soft turn to the bilges, a firm or full midsection, or a hard bilge with V-bottom and chines, by which a yacht can be made tender or stiff.

The accompanying diagrams are shown to illustrate how important these factors can be in achieving sail carrying power and ultimate stability. In A1, a typical midsection is shown of an old-time cutter, with narrow beam for her length, slack bilges and a deep ballast keel. This type had little *initial* stability and tended to heel at first very easily,

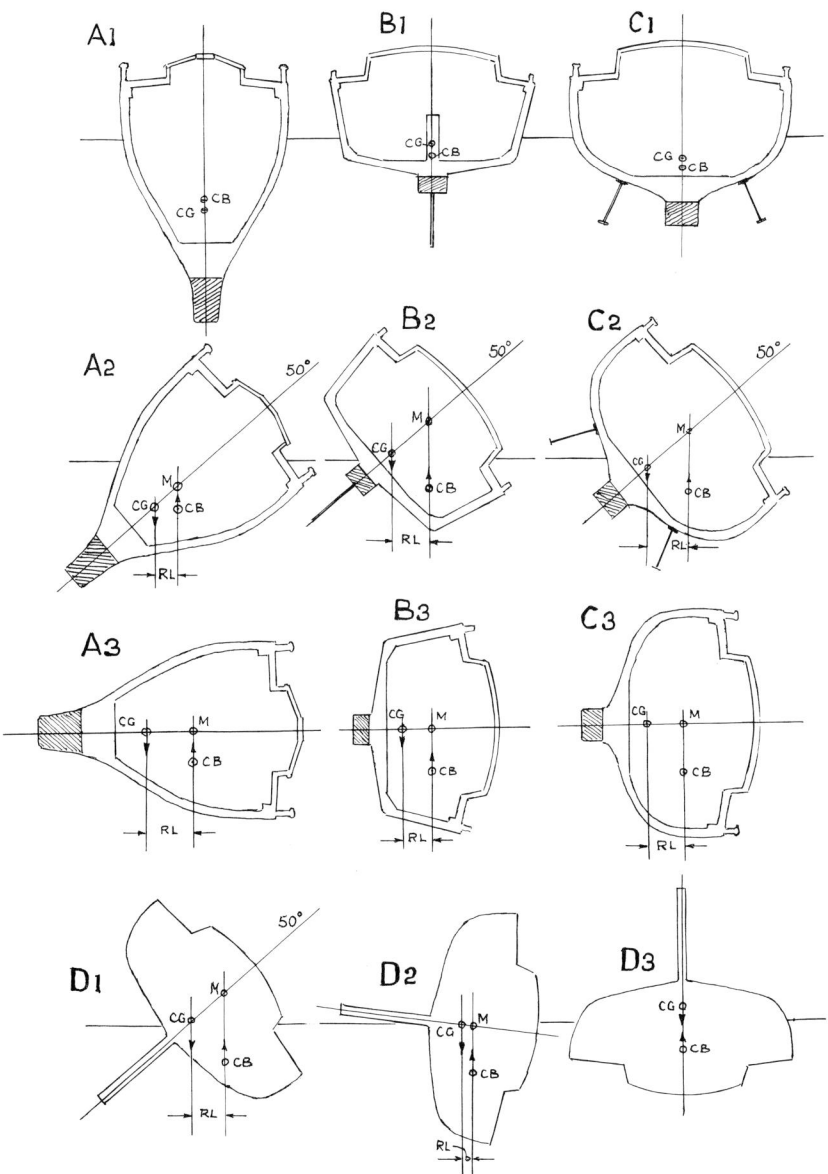

Relative heeling stability of four diverse types of yacht.

until the pendulum effect of the iron or lead keel began to take effect.

When the heeling reached an angle of something like 50 degrees (A2), the righting effect of the keel became such that it would be difficult to make her heel further. If caught in a rising gale with too much canvas aloft the yacht might lie over to 60 or 70 degrees with water up to the skylight, but by now the wind would be escaping over the heads of the sails, and it would need a great sea breaking over her ever to lay her flat (at 90 degrees heel) as in A3. If she were lost (as in the case of the extreme plank-on-edge *Oona, see Chapter III*) it would be through the loss of her keel, or flooding through an open or smashed skylight or hatch.

The stability of this yacht can be seen in the relative positions of the centre of gravity of the whole vessel (CG, where her weight presses her down in the water) and the centre of buoyancy (CB, or point at which the centre of the water displaced by the hull is buoying her up). When the yacht is upright (A1) the CG is directly below the CB, but when heeled to, say, 50 degrees (A2) the CB has shifted some distance to leeward, creating a righting lever (RL) which resists the heeling power of the sails, and the yacht is said to have 'found her bearings'. If forced over to 90 degrees (AE) the CB shifts even further to leeward, increasing the righting effect, RL.

The point at which the vertical line from CB meets the centre line of the hull which passes through CG is called the metacentre (M), whose height above the CG is a measure of any vessel's inherent stability. In big ships a high metacentre causes rapid rolling, and in square rig days a deeply laden ship with a high M could roll her masts out in a calm swell. In passenger ships a *low* M is aimed at so as to give a slow, easy roll for the comfort of all on board; but cases have been known for the M to be so little above the CG of the ship that the vessel has been unstable. The loss of the passenger liner *Waratah* off the West African coast in 1909 was due to her inherent instability, and there are many ships afloat today, from trawlers to big freighters, which are so near to being unstable that they have to be handled with great care in bad weather: while many have just disappeared.

Compared with the deep draft yacht in A, a very different type is represented in B1. This is a conventional V-bottom or chine centreboarder with an outside iron keel. The midsection is near to that of a small barge, and has great initial stability. This means that as she heels she immerses a large amount of her hull on the lee side while exposing a roughly equal mount on the windward side. This type of boat would normally sail at small angles of heel, say 10 to 15 degrees, but if forced over to, say, 50 degrees (B2) it will be seen how her CB has shifted to leeward and formed between the points M and CG a powerful righting lever (RL). Even laid flat (B3) or 90 degrees heel there is still an adequate righting lever (RL) to toss her back on her feet, if she has not already shipped enough water to sink her. The outside iron keel, however, would probably bring her back even with the cabin awash, and a complete capsize and total loss of a boat of this type is very rare.

Another type of shallow draft yacht is shown in C1; a fairly conventional round bilge cruiser with firm midsections, bilge keels and a central iron ballast keel. With a beam of at least one-third of the LWL she would have much initial stability and sail generally at small angles of heel. If in strong gusts she is laid over to 50 degrees (C2) it will be seen how far the CB has moved to leeward, meeting M far above CG, thus giving a strong righting lever (RL). Such a boat could be relied on to get back on her feet if ever she was laid flat or even rolled by a breaking sea, and represents a notably safe yacht for shoal water or offshore cruising.

The midsection of a typical Class 3 ocean racer is shown in D1 for comparison with the cruiser type, and perhaps for those who ask for more excitement from their boats. With its wide flat hull and light displacement this machine has an adequate righting lever (RL) when heeled to 50 degrees. But in conditions when wind and seas force her over to a complete knockdown (D2) the CG and M are brought so close together that there is very little righting tendancy left. Almost inevitably there will be a flip over with the mast pointing to the seabed and the keel upwards (D3). And with the CB (a doubtful position as the yacht is almost bound now to have a fair quantity of water in her) balanced in line with the CG this is how the yacht will remain until she either fills up and sinks, or a breaking sea flips her keel over and she turns upright again.

This unhappy situation is how so many of the smaller yachts behaved in the violent conditions encountered in the 1979 Fastnet Race when 15 lives were lost. It stands as an indictment of the rating rules in use at the time that such yachts should be built and entered for a tough offshore race.

* * *

No doubt many yachtsmen have sailed in yachts which have been of similar type one to another, yet have found it difficult to explain why they can be so different in their behaviour at sea. It is an age old phenomenon, for was it not King Solomon who spoke of the wonders of the world and gave one as 'the way of a ship in the midst of the sea'? Most yachtsmen will have noticed that amongst vessels which are alleged to have been built to the same designs, perhaps in the same yard, one will prove faster, quicker in stays, even drier in a seaway than her sistership. It is not always due to a better helmsman, yachts of a single class can vary in their performance under the same conditions.

It might be put down to Sod's Law, but even machines which are supposed to be identical are rarely exactly the same in operation. We have all met rogue cars and good cars of the same make and model; while on railways in steam days, locomotives of the same class, reputedly identical and built by the same men at the same works, have shown differing idiosyncracies. Drivers and firemen have noted how much their behaviour can differ one from another. 'You have to get to know this old girl and her ways', an old driver once told me of one class. 'If you don't she'll make your life a misery.'

In yachts, even in these days of production in GRP from identical moulds, no two seem to be exactly alike. The dispostion of weights on board play a surprisingly important part in affecting a boat's behaviour. If one owner, for instance, decides to carry an extra 40 metres of chain cable for the bow anchor stowed right forward, and carries his kedge and warps in addition in the forepeak; adds an extra water tank forward for the shower in the heads, and stows some of the heavy stores in the fo'cs'le lockers, the ship will naturally tend to trim an inch or two by the head. To correct this the owner might hopefully add extra water and fuel tanks aft (with long distance cruising in view) and additional batteries for all the electrical appliances and navigational aids on board.

These weights towards the stern might well balance those forward, and when at rest the yacht might float on the designed waterline, if perhaps an inch or two below these marks. All looks well, but at sea the difference will show in her motion. These weights concentrated in the ends of the ship are spread out from the point amidships about which the vessel pitches, exerting as they are lifted and dropped a powerful fulcrum, so that she will alternatively plunge deeply into the troughs and drop her stern. It might make her a very wet ship, but inevitably her speed potential in a seaway will be impaired.

In contrast, an identical yacht (from the same moulds) whose owner has thoughtfully kept the principal weights — engine installation, fuel, water tanks, batteries, ship's stores, ground tackle — as near amidships as practicable, and the ends as light as possible, will be much livelier in a seaway, drier, quicker in stays, and probably lighter on the helm. The yacht designer has to be fully aware of the effects of this disposal of weights in the hull and on deck, even if the owner subsequently undoes much of his fine calculating, and this is why the keen racing chaps take so much care to carry no unnecessary weight in the bow or stern of their high-tech machines.

For those who are interested in transferring the lines to paper of either their own yacht, or for posterity the hull lines and rig of, say, a traditional fishing vessel or small commercial boat, I have added some notes in Appendix 1. The methods described of taking off a boat's lines are quite straightforward, even if they might appear somewhat involved, but with one or two willing helpers the job does not take long.

In days gone by it was the custom for yachting magazines to publish a set of lines with the description of new yachts. This policy has died out in recent years, partly because it is claimed that few present day yachtsmen have learnt to read the significance of a

Jappa, *one of the Bawley class versions of the Cockler series built by Johnson & Jago in the 1950s.*

yacht's lines, but principally because modern photocopying processes have enabled anyone to reproduce published drawings enlarged to any convenient scale for his/her own use.

It should be understood that all plans of yachts (likewise those of ships, machinery, houses, public buildings) printed in magazines and books are the copyright of their designers or architects, and to 'lift' them for building purposes without obtaining the designer's permission or paying his fee is illegal. Yet this is not always understood and it is regrettable to record that the habit of enlarging printed plans from a magazine or book and using them to build a new yacht has become prevalent amongst the less scrupulous in some countries overseas.

In the years since my first attempts on the drawing board to produce designs of the kind of small cruising yacht that appealed to me — and hopefully to others as well — to more recent times when it became clear that the eyes could no longer take the strain of working in fine lines on tracing paper, I find I have logged together 140 different yacht designs. Of these something over one hundred sets of plans have been completed and yachts built to them in various parts of the world; while others have remained projects only on the drawing board and not proceeded with.

SIXTY YEARS A YACHT DESIGNER

Counting the numbers built of the Bawley, Cockler, Barcarole, Eventide, Waterwitch, Golden Hind and other classes, it has been estimated that to date (1987) a total of some 1600 yachts have been produced to Griffiths designs over the years, many of them scattered around the Seven Seas. Out of this collection I have selected a number of the more successful designs for inclusion in the following pages to illustrate the type of uncomplicated cruising yacht I have tried to encourage over all these years while engaged in editorial work and the production of a number of books. It is gratifying to think that many of these little ships have made their owners very happy indeed.

As we approach the twenty first century the profession of yacht designing is being completely revolutionised by modern technology, just as it is in the building of ships. I have to admit that I am filled with admiration for the strides made in the design and performance of modern yachts and for the coming generations of designers with their grasp of all that the use of computers and processors has to offer them. The concept of the fast, planing cruising yacht with its easy to handle gear and sparkling performance is exciting, and only just round the corner.

SEAWAY

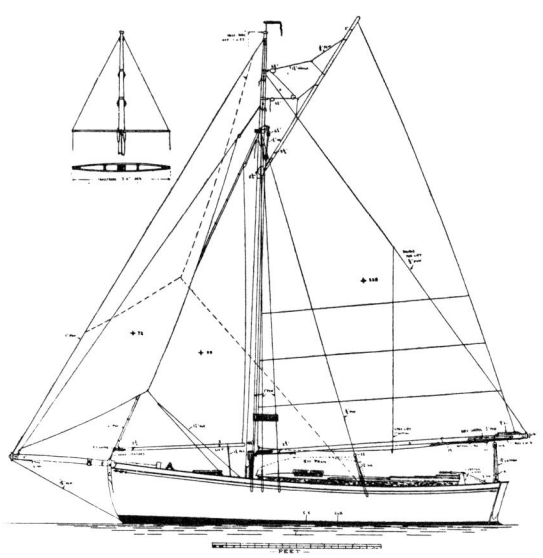

LOA	28.0ft
LWL	26.0ft
BEAM	8.5ft
DRAFT	4.0ft
DISPLACEMENT	6.64 tons
IRON KEEL	2.75 tons
WKG SAIL AREA	495 sq ft
THAMES M'MT	7½ tons

SEAWAY WAS ONE of a series of transom sterned cutter designs which ranged from 25 feet to 30 feet overall (excluding bowsprit). The owner of this 28 foot cutter wanted a sturdy cruising boat to keep in Portsmouth Harbour, in which he could sail single-handed in the Channel safely in almost any weather.

In a previous boat he had been completely swept by a sea, and in *Seaway* he asked that the cockpit might be covered by a wide sliding hatch which could be pulled aft, when required, to allow only sufficient opening for the helmsman. With this hatch completely closed and bolted the yacht was fairly secure against marauders when unattended. The draft was

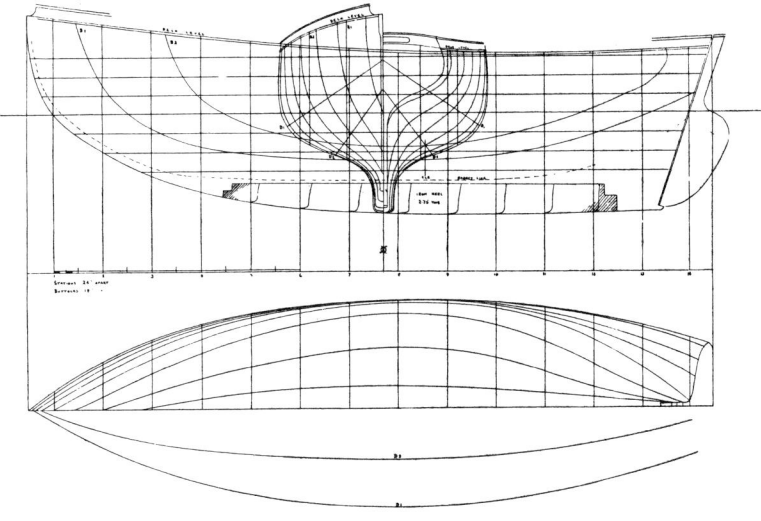

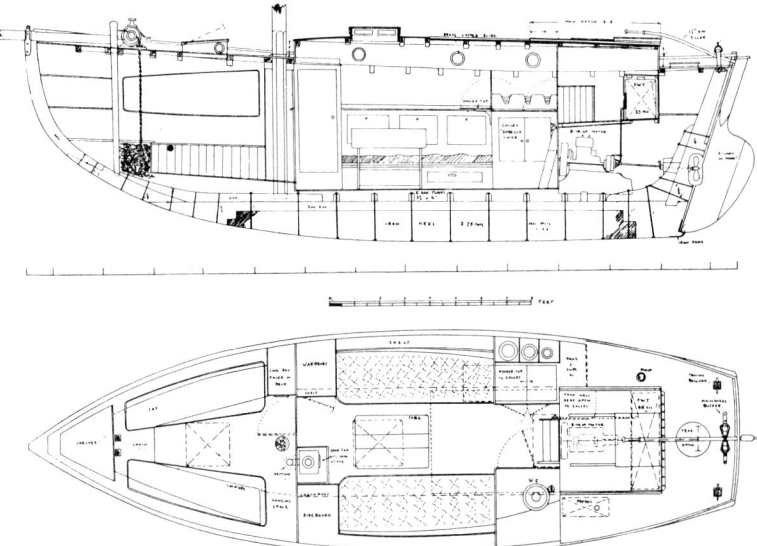

limited to four feet to enable the boat to sail into shallow places like Chichester and Poole and many of the harbours of Brittany.

Seaway was strongly built in larch on oak frames at Portsmouth in 1930, and with her firm bilge sections she proved a stiff boat and difficult to put her lee rail under in most breezy weather. Two 6-foot 3-inch settee berths in the cabin and two pipecots in the fo'cs'le slept four when required, while home comfort in off season was provided by a small coal stove in the saloon. There was five feet headroom in the fo'cs'le and 5 feet 8 inches in the saloon under coachroof beams. A 10hp 2-cylinder motor gave a cruising speed of about five knots. She was lost through a petrol fire a few years later.

IONIA

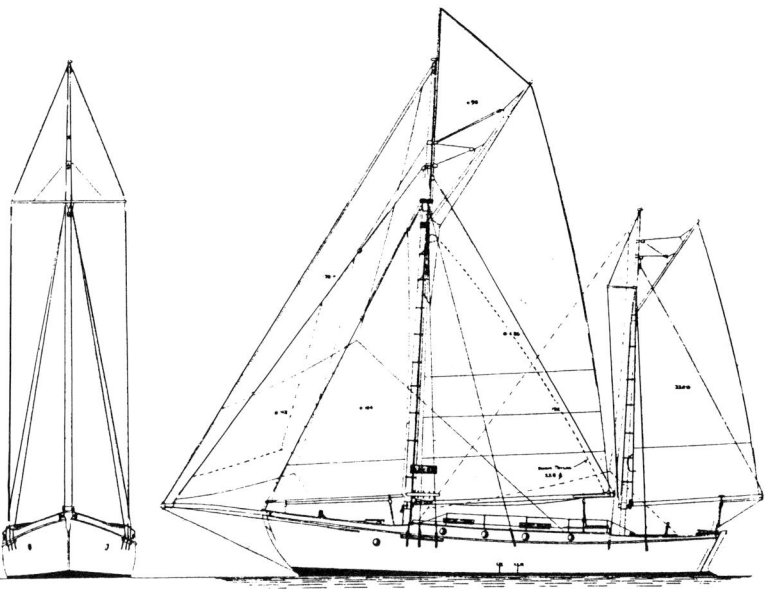

LOA	45.5ft
LWL	39.0ft
BEAM	13.0ft
DRAFT	4.0ft
CB DOWN	8.0ft
DISPLACEMENT	15.7 tons
BALLAST KEEL	3.75 tons
WKG SAIL AREA	1,062 sq ft
THAMES M'MT	29 tons

BUILT TO A high standard by Egyptian shipwrights at Alexandria in 1933, this design aimed at a truly shallow draft centreboarder which could ride out the worst the Mediterranean was likely to hurl at her, and yet to be able to sail up the Nile to the shoal waters at the First Cataract. Although planned, no auxiliary engine was installed, and she was comfortably steered by tiller.

In this design, with the intention of giving the hull great strength and plenty of air space below decks in the hot Khamseen winds, I introduced the form of deck construction I later adopted for many of my smaller shoal draft yachts. In this the main deck was raised from the mainmast to the fore end of the cockpit with no break in the deck beams for waterways. With no coachroof and fewer deck joints there were fewer places where leaks could develop in the hot Egyptian sun.

In the accommodation layout there were two pipecots forward for the Egyptian crew, with crew's heads, washbasin, galley and coal store for the saloon stove — a necessity when cruising in winter off the Greek and Turkish coasts. The built-up hardwood centreboard was weighted with

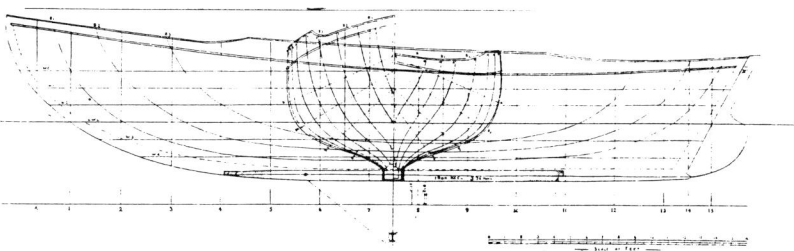

180 lb to give it negative buoyancy while making it easy to work with a simple purchase.

The saloon had both settee and pilot berths to starboard and port respectively, and swivel chairs to the table, while to starboard a writing desk for the owner's archaeological work, which could also double up as a chart table. The cruising that *Ionia* carried out in the Aegean, amongst the Greek and Turkish islands and in the Ionian Sea was later to prove of great value. At the time of the German advance on the Middle East in 1942 her owner was able to give the British naval authorities in Alexandria data on harbours and anchorages where U-boats might lurk which were to be of much assistance to the Allies.

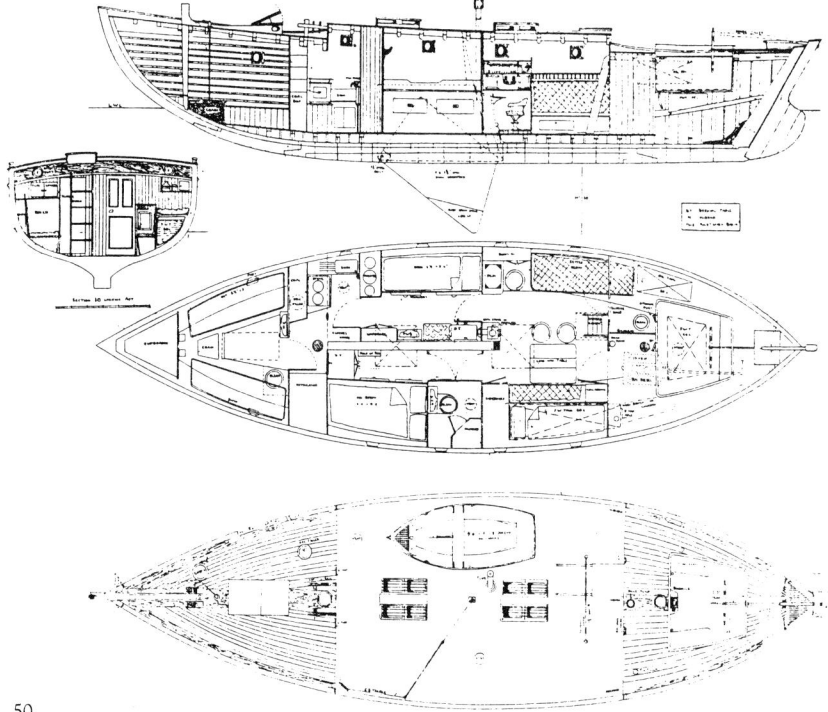

WILD LONE II

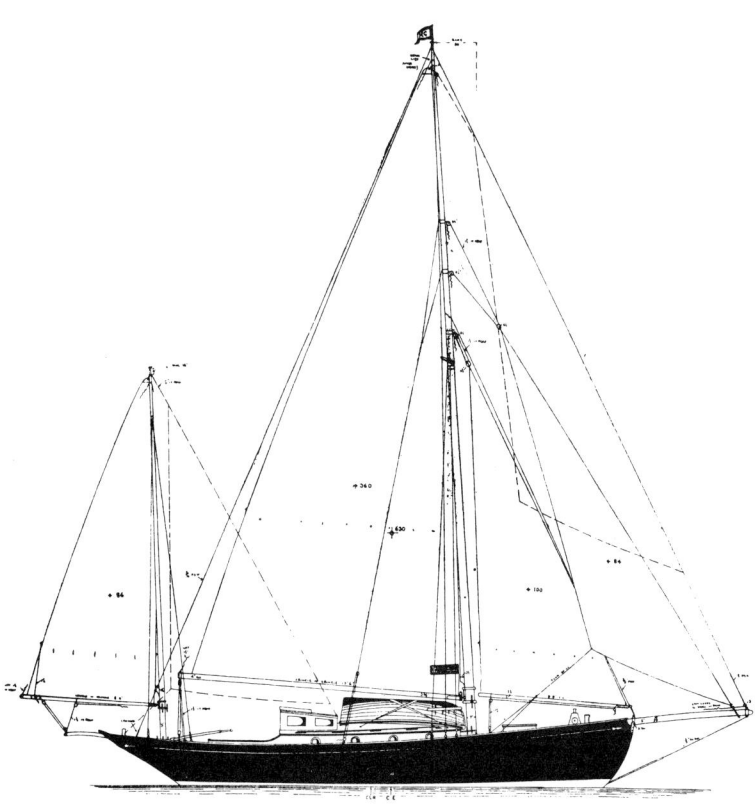

Loa	35.7ft
Lwl	28.0ft
Beam	9.3ft
Draft	4.9ft
Displacement	8.25 tons
Iron keel	3.10 tons
Wkg sail area	630 sq ft
Thames m'mt	10 tons

THIS DESIGN sprang from an urge to combine a thoroughly conventional cruising hull of the period with a reasonably proportioned yawl rig which would enable the yacht to handle under almost any combination of sails. *Wild Lone* II's hull with its long straight keel and deep forefoot was purely traditional, and indeed old fashioned with its heavy displacement and, to today's eyes, deficient freeboard. The easy sections in the bow were matched by the fine run aft to the narrow counter, and condusive to an easily driven hull; but as one critic observed when he first clapped eyes on her: 'Like Cassius, she hath a lean and hungry look!'

Wild Lone II was built by King and Sons at Pin Mill in 1935, and proved as light on the helm with an agreeably easy motion when beating into a chop as one might expect. With the Wykeham Martin jib rolled up and mizzen stowed she would balance well under main and staysail, and reefs in the main did not appear to affect the helm as the wind increased still further.

Like most long keel yawls, handling her in narrow places under mizzen and jib alone took patience and some judgement, for with her weight she

would carry her way for some distance and would need a wide circle to come round. The real value of the mizzen proved more in its absence — stowed as a first reef — than in its limited driving force, and indeed it has long been debatable whether the extra gear, expense and windage of a yawl's mizzen on a displacement hull was ever worth while. When a sister ship, *Jorrocks* II, was built the following year to the same set of plans by Harris at Burnham for Sir Carne Rasch, the mizzen was omitted. On one or two trial sails *Jorrocks* as a Bermuda cutter proved a better boat than her yawl sister when on a wind, and certainly no slower with the wind free, for the area of *Wild Lone*'s mizzen had been added to the mainsail.

For many years *Jorrocks* sailed to Holland with the owner and his equally elderly paid hand from the Colne, and after Sir Carne died she continued in her berth at Wivenhoe up to the time of writing (1987), a black hulled representative of a bygone type. *Wild Lone* II had a spell in the Western Isles under Scottish ownership until bought by the Wallace Clark family who based her at the little harbour of Portrush near their home in Northern Ireland. Renamed *Wild Goose* she has cruised

WILD LONE II

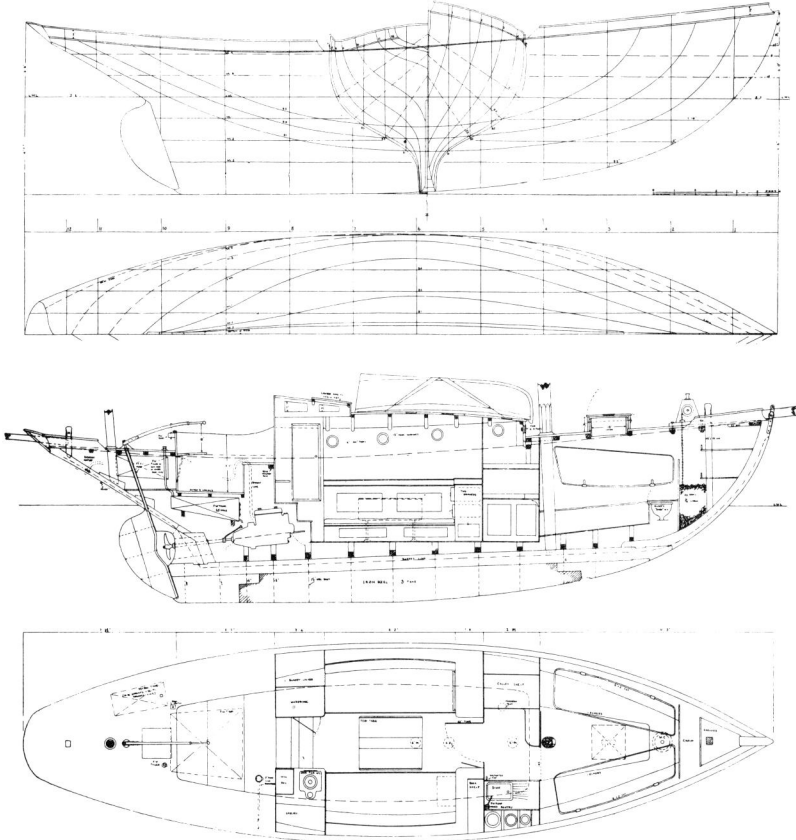

extensively to the Mediterranean and back as well as around the Emerald Isle's coast and to Scotland, and despite a few modernising additions she has retained her original yawl rig. Wallace Clark has described one of his cruises in her in his book *Sailing Round Ireland* (Batsford, London, 1976) which has all the poetic description to be expected from an Irishman of his beloved coast. She has evidently proved a very happy little ship.

LONE GULL I

LOA	28.5 ft
LWL	25.0 ft
BEAM	10.0 ft
DRAFT	3.2 ft
AND	6.0 ft
DISPLACEMENT	5.45 tons
WKG SAIL AREA	480 sq ft
BUILDERS	Johnson & Jago, Leigh-on Sea, 1938
THAMES M'MT	10 tons

AS A RESULT of the influence of American centreboard design *Lone Gull* I was given a bold breadth of 10 feet on a 25-foot waterline, together with a built-up oak centreboard. The fore end of the case was flush with the cabin sole boards, the raised after end with lifting chain forming a fore and aft bulkhead for the galley to port.

This proved a good arrangement for the accommodation, but necessitated the complication of an offset engine (a Gray Four-22 petrol motor) driving the central propeller shaft through a silent chain housed in a box. The dinette table to starboard, with roll-up root berth above, was I think another mistake: the traditional two settee berths with central table has so often proved the better arrangement.

Trouble with leaks along the joints of the decks and coamings were difficult to cure, as the coamings were high ones and the mast, stepped on the top of the keel, tended to move the cabin top from side to side

LONE GULL I

in breezy weather however much the rigging screws were set up. A mast stepped on deck, as in modern practice, avoids these wringing strains. This fundamental weakness of a large coachroof and the trouble with deck joint leaks were factors which led me to adopt the raised midship deck, as I had fitted to the large centreboarder *Ionia*, to many of my subsequent shallow draft designs.

Apart from its very much stronger construction the raised deck on any shallow hull adds greatly to the sense of space in the cabin in a small yacht, while avoiding that cricked neck posture one assumes beneath the side deck carlines in many cabin top boats.

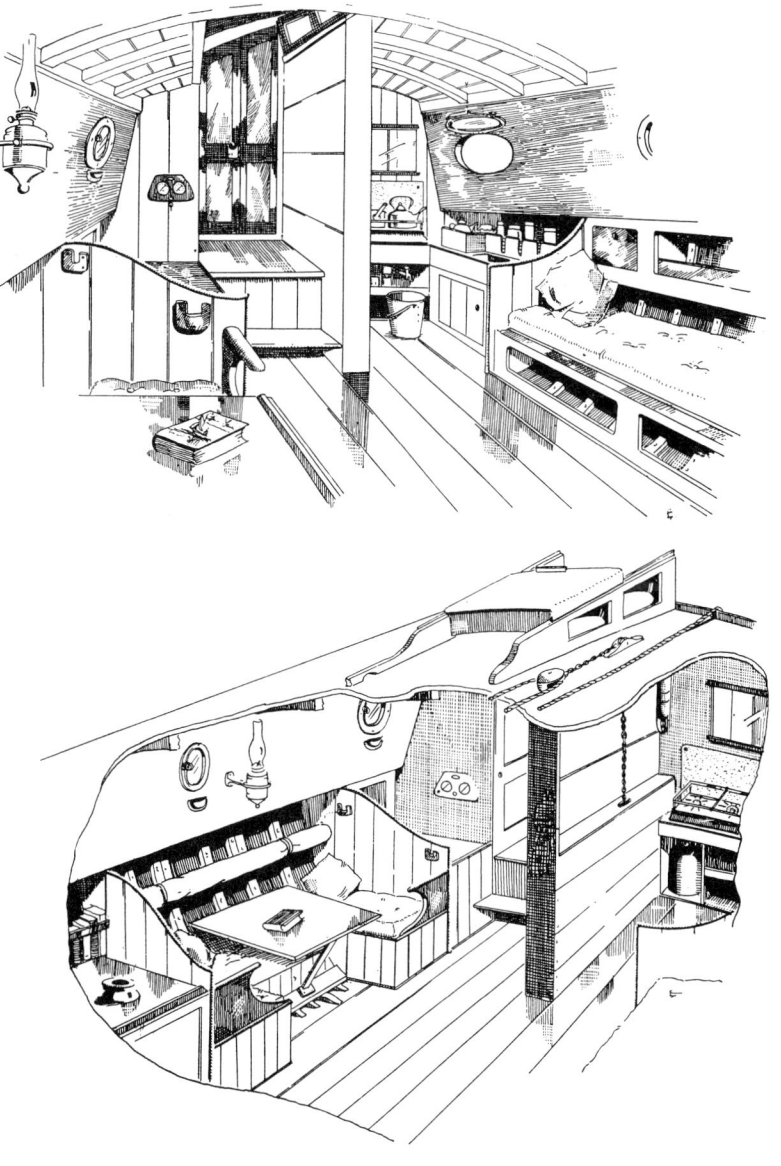

LONE GULL I

Lone Gull I's Bermuda cutter rig with short bowsprit and the jib as well as the foresail hanked to stays was conventional enough for its day. The last gaff rigged yacht I owned had been Nightfall, a light weight shoal draft cutter built in 1910, which I had sold in 1935, and I have never owned a gaffer since. But I still can enjoy *watching* the dedicated gaffers sailing their picturesque smacks and bawleys and old time cutters with all their traditional blocks and tackle and pully-hauly and artistic curves in the sails like an old time marine painting.

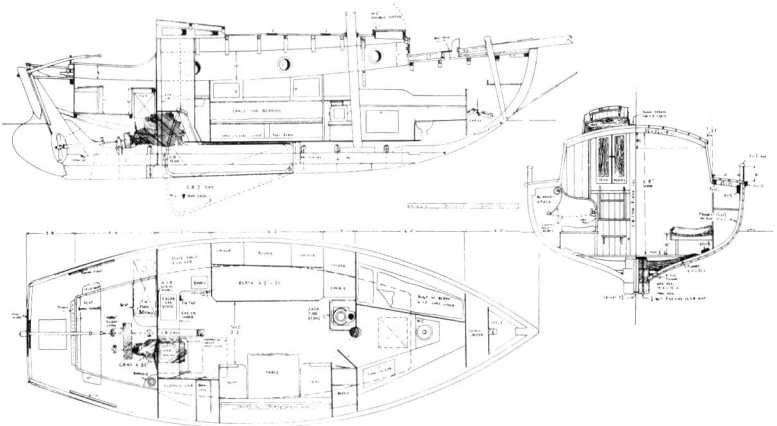

JULIANA

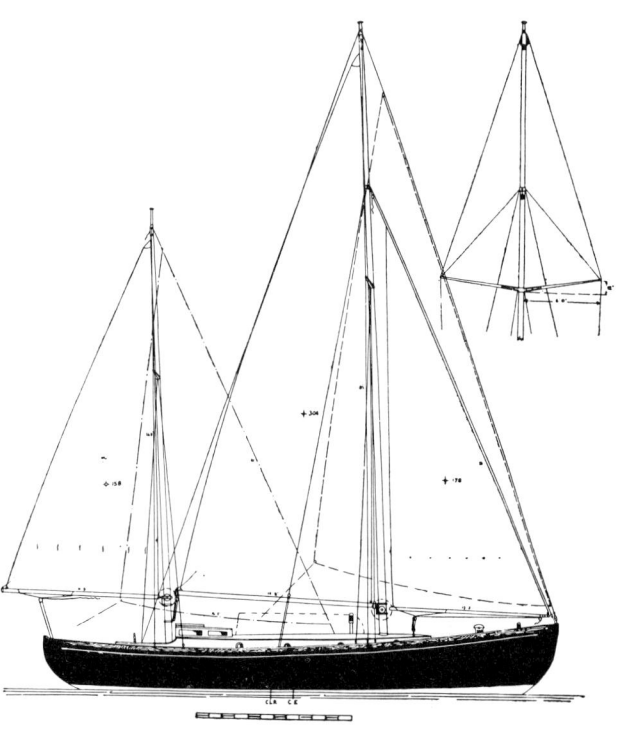

LOA	40.0ft
LWL	34.2ft
BEAM	11.5ft
DRAFT	4.5ft and 7.0 ft
DISPLACEMENT	11.6 tons
WKG SAIL AREA	690 sq ft
LIGHT WEATHER	1305 sq ft

AN ORDER WAS received from a client in Holland for a comfortable 40 foot centreboarder with maximum hull draft of 4.5 feet to suit the Continental waterways, but to be capable of long distance blue water voyages when the time came. The owner favoured a canoe stern with inboard mounted rudder and geared wheel steering, and no bowsprit to the ketch rig.

Juliana emerged as a result, and as the plans reproduced here indicate she had a neat looking hull with a moderate sheer, while her ends looked as though they balanced. With her full sections and (by today's standards) heavy displacement, her 11.5-foot beam gave her a powerful hull with impressive space below decks. With 30-inch wide side decks and a low coachroof from forward of the mainmast to the cockpit there was 6.3 feet headroom over the cabin sole.

Normally, the crew was to consist only of the owner and his wife, both experienced seamen and navigators, with only the occasional guest or two. The forepeak was accordingly given over to simple toilet requirements and boat stores, with a fold up pipe berth for emergencies. The owners' two-berth cabin was adjacent. The case for the wooden centreboard did not intrude above the saloon sole, while the after end, raised to the deck and housing the lifting chain, formed part of the fore and aft bulkhead between the galley and oilskins locker and the engine room.

JULIANA

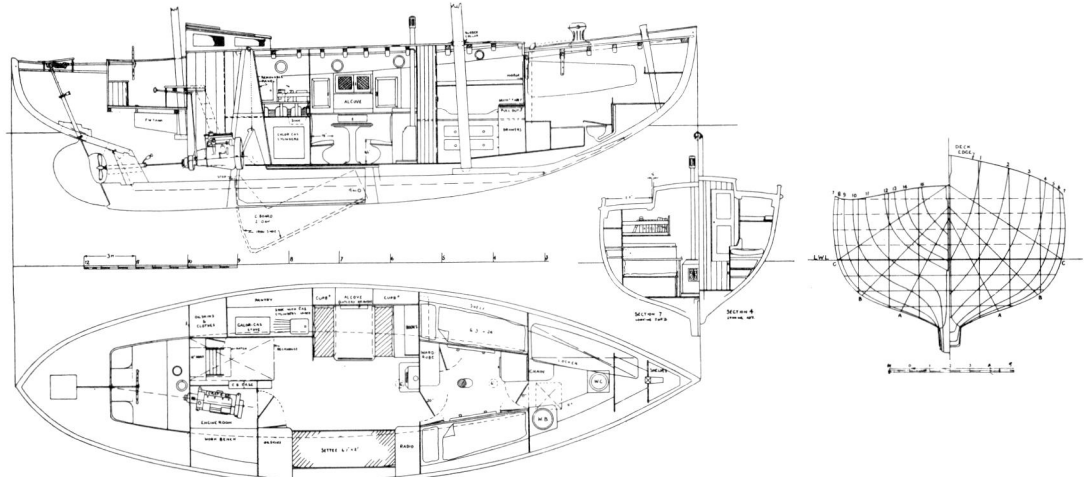

Carimon

Carimon

Here there was full headroom with a useful work bench.

In place of the contemporary yacht windlass the anchor gear was handled by a geared capstan from which the chain dropped into its locker below. The old fashioned upright capstan with its two-handle operation had many points in its favour for the cruising yacht, since its handles were at a more convenient height above deck for working than the lever of the usual small windlass; two men with a handle each could put far more strain on the cable than they could with the normal winch handles, while for warping the windlass with its vertical drum can take a warp from any angle round the ship without the need for snatchblocks. Neat electric windlasses for the larger yachts and for the smaller boats shiny chromium winches at surprising prices took over in the bright lights at boat shows, and the faithful capstan became an obsolete item. I think it regrettable.

A near sister ship to *Juliana*, but with a raking transom stern, a different cabin layout and stemhead Bermuda cutter (or slutter) rig was built, largely of teak, in Singapore, in 1939. *Carimon*, as she was named, had the same 40-foot by 11.5-foot with 4.5-foot draft ex-CB measurements, and according to her owner's reports she turned out a lovely, sturdy little ship which was a delight to handle. Cruises through the Java Sea and the Macassar Strait to the Philippines and (who knows?) on to the islands of the Pacific were planned for when time became available, but the fall of Singapore intervened, and unhappily the little ship was sunk by the Japanese while trying to escape in 1942.

CENTREBOARDS

MY FIRST ATTEMPT at designing a centreboard (or plate) which would not divide a small yacht's cabin in two with an obtrusive case was the one I fitted to the 27.5-foot *Wind Song*, launched at Portsmouth in 1929 and shown here in the original accommodation layout plan. The forward arm of the plate, like a half open knife blade, was worked through a slot in the foredeck by a 4:1 tackle led aft to the cockpit.

On the whole this worked very well, and while the boat had her original cutter rig with the jib on a bowsprit she carried no more weather helm than normal with a shallow hull. But when in later years she was converted to Bermuda sloop rig without a bowsprit, she showed her dislike by becoming somewhat hard on the helm in anything of a breeze, and needed tiller lines to act as a relieving purchase.

An unexpected advantage of the position of *Wind Song*'s centreplate when turning to windward against a tide and running aground, was that it did not allow the ship's head at once to pay off inshore, but held her steady in the tide. With jib sheets let fly smartly and helm held down she would begin to pivot on the foot of her plate and weathercock into the tide until she came head to wind. With the jib now held aback and the plate hauled up a few inches, she would be away again within the minute and heading back into the channel. Smartly carried out this operation could dispense with leadline or echosounder.

A variation on the *Wind Song* arrangement was adopted for the *Cockler* class and is shown in the general arrangement plan here. This boat was 25 feet on deck, 22 feet waterline with 8 feet beam and 2.9 feet draft with plate raised, and followed somewhat vaguely the lines of the older cockle bawleys then to be found lying in Leigh Creek. The builders were Seacraft

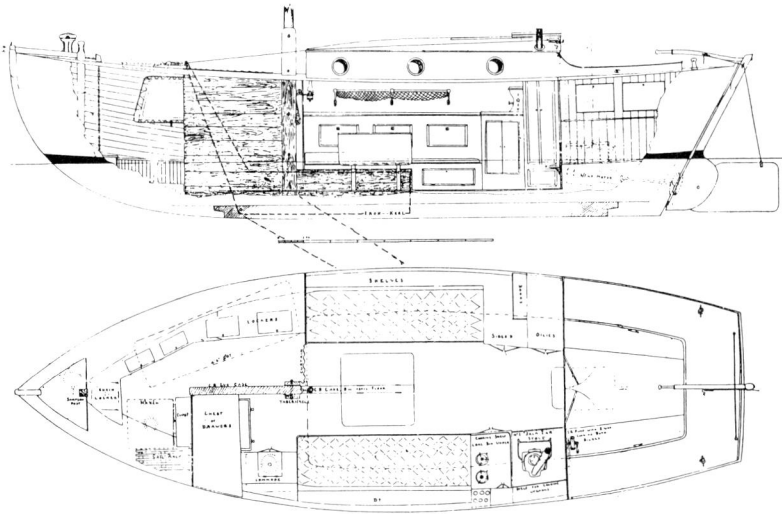

CENTREBOARDS

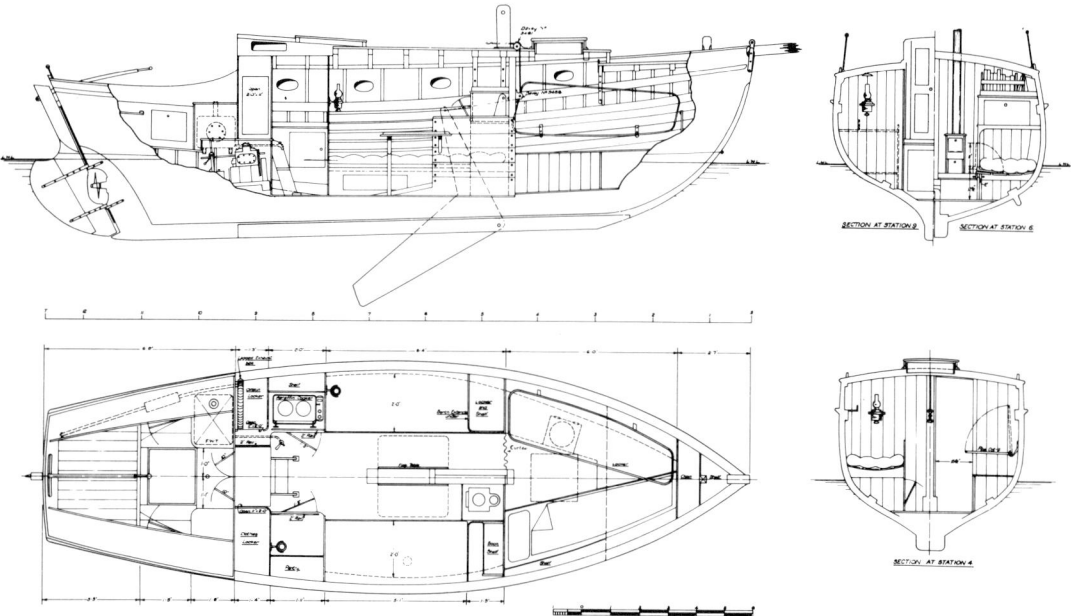

and Co (now no longer in business) and like *Wind Song*'s the centreboard was of mild steel plate and shaped like the knifeblade. This time its pivot point was abaft the mast, and the upper arm worked through a slot in the case to a tackle led through a hooded sheave on deck aft to the cockpit.

This arrangement seemed to work very well, and the position of the plate's leading edge relative to the sail plan appeared about right, as these little boats sailed well and did not gripe or pull on the helm unduly. Because in rough going the water tended to slop up through the slot in the centreboard case (despite preventive stuffing) and make for a wet cabin sole, the case was later carried up to the deck with a removable inspection panel inserted for access to the plate and its lifting gear. A number of these little boats were built at Leigh-on-Sea and in different parts of the world, but a keel version drawing 3.6 feet, and known as the Bawley, came to be built in larger numbers.

A wooden built-up centreboard was introduced in the next design, two of which were built alongside each other in the Seacraft yard, and became known as the *Tringa* class. The owners both favoured the lifeboat or Scottish type stern for reasons of being able to part the following seas when running before a gale. I have personnaly never been convinced of the advantages of this type of stern — effective enough in a slow moving lifeboat — for a sailing yacht, which needs a good deal of bearing (or buoyancy) at the quarters to hold up under the power of the mainsail. And in planning these boats I found the same effect of the nipped-in quarters and lack of buoyancy as well as space around the cockpit as I had met when designing the 30-footer *Loon*.

The centreboard with its raised arm aft, however, fitted in well with the layout aft around the portside galley, and was easy and very light to work and had sufficient ballast to make it sink. The arrangement is clearly shown in the accompanying construction drawings of *Tringa*, whose overall measurements were 27.8 feet on deck, 23.0 feet waterline, 8.4 feet beam and 3.0 feet draft and 5.6 feet with centreboard down.

These little sloops with their various sistership sailed well and were well balanced when underway with reasonable handheld weather helm. Like all my shoal draft designs they had sufficient weight on their iron ballast keels to bring them back on their feet if ever rolled over or laid flat in a knockdown. One of the class, indeed, did just that when making for Ostende in a rising southwesterly gale on her beam under a close-reefed mainsail only. A freak sea broke right over her, smothering the skipper at the helm, and rolled her down until the sail was in the water. But she lifted herself back before the cockpit had time to become flooded — and carried on sailing. The owner's daughter, who was resting in her lee berth in the foc's'le, was totally unaware of any untoward antics happening outside, until told afterwards!

What proved a generally successful follow up of the *Tringa* line of boats was the *Barcarole* class. Over the years Seacraft and Co were to build ten of these boats, all inevitably with minor variations to meet each owner's requirements. A little larger than their predecessors the Barcaroles were generally 29.2 feet on deck, 24.0 feet waterline, 8.4 feet beam and 3.2 feet draft with raking transom sterns.

All these yachts had the raised midship deck with the beams carried unbroken from beam shelf to beam shelf, except in the way of the main hatchway and forehatch. The result was that their interiors struck visitors as remarkable for their sense of space and airiness and sitting headroom above the settees. The strength inherent in this flush deck type of construction was borne out when a boat of this class was caught between two canal barges in a French lock. Although she was badly squeezed amidships, none of the deck beams gave way, and after repairs at a yard she was able to complete her cruise. With a conventional coachroof with side decks it would probably have been a different story.

The Cockler type of centreplate, of ½ inch steel, was planned originally for this class, with the lifting gear concealed inside the upward extension of the case, which had the usual inspection panel, and led aft to the cockpit. The vagaries of centreboard boats encourage ingenuity on the owner's part in dealing with them, and one is having the plate jammed up inside the case after the boat has settled on, say, a half-tide mooring for a number of tides. Mud and shells tend to get packed solid in the keel slot and only a bar, used as a lever from the deck beams, is likely to shift it. If this will not move the plate, a short length of an old band saw may

CENTREBOARDS

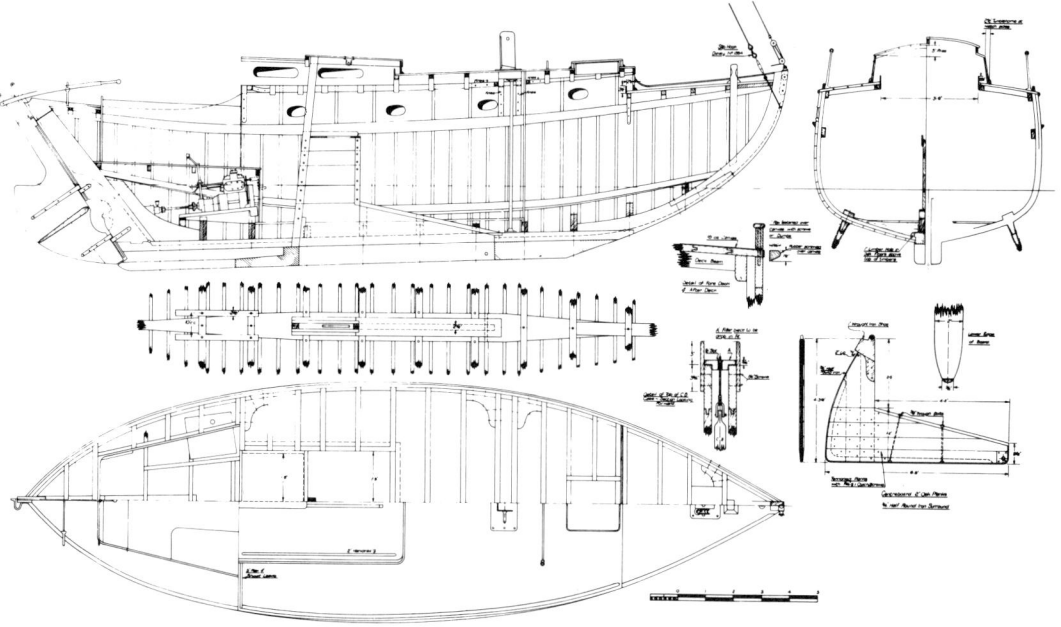

be used to cut the mud round the plate. Both are useful tools in a centreboarder's inventory.

To get at the plate while the yacht is still afloat some part of the case *must* be taken away above the waterline, otherwise it means the yacht will have to be put ashore, or on a slip, and that can be an intolerable nuisance just to free a jammed plate. This is why I have always insisted on bringing some part of the centreboard case well above the waterline with easily removable access hatch or panel. (What, *always*? Well, nearly always.) Years ago I was commissioned to design a centreboarder by a west country firm for quantity production in GRP. Unfortunately, the directors insisted that no part of the centreboard case should extend above the level of the cabin sole, as they held that buyers just would not tolerate an obstruction in an otherwise very spacious saloon. I accepted this with reluctance after some discussion, and the result was a shallow rectangular steel plate housed in the keel underneath the floorboards, worked by a single stainless steel wire led in a tube to the deck winch, and with no stop to prevent the plate falling right down should the lifting tackle part. As the plate was inaccessible from inside the boat while she was afloat, the builders reluctantly accepted a second pipe at the after end with a screw cap above waterline, which would take a rod to poke the plate down when it refused to lower of its own weight. It was not my idea of a satisfactory installation, and I only hope the boats of this class kept off the ground and had no trouble with jammed plates.

The question of how to deal with barnacles and marine borers inside a wooden case is no problem. A practical dodge is, at least once a season,

CENTREBOARDS

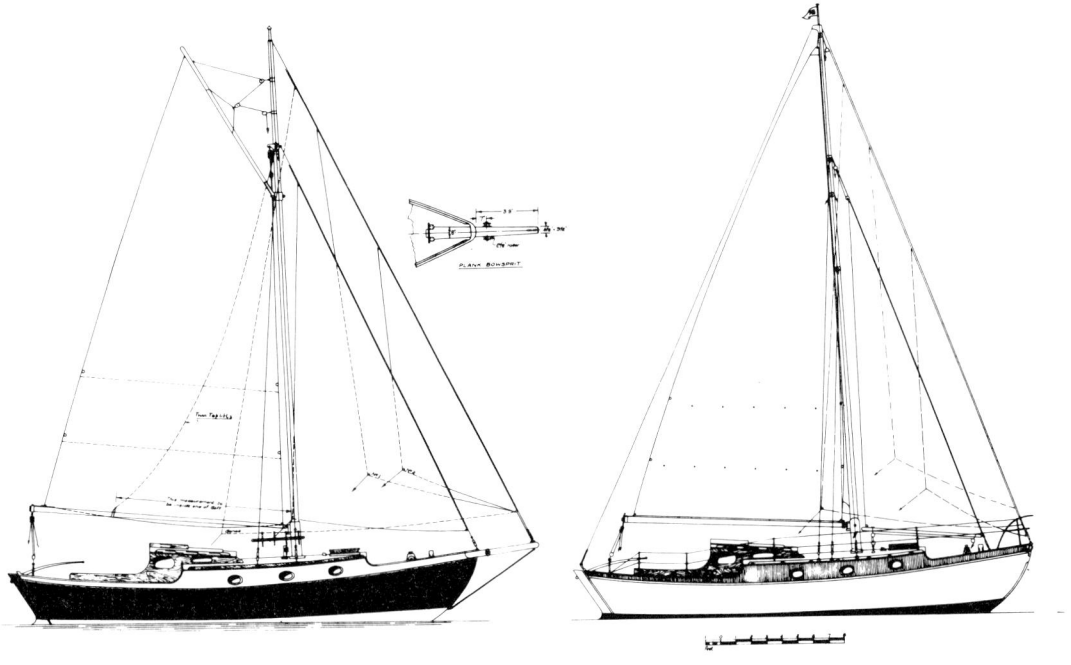

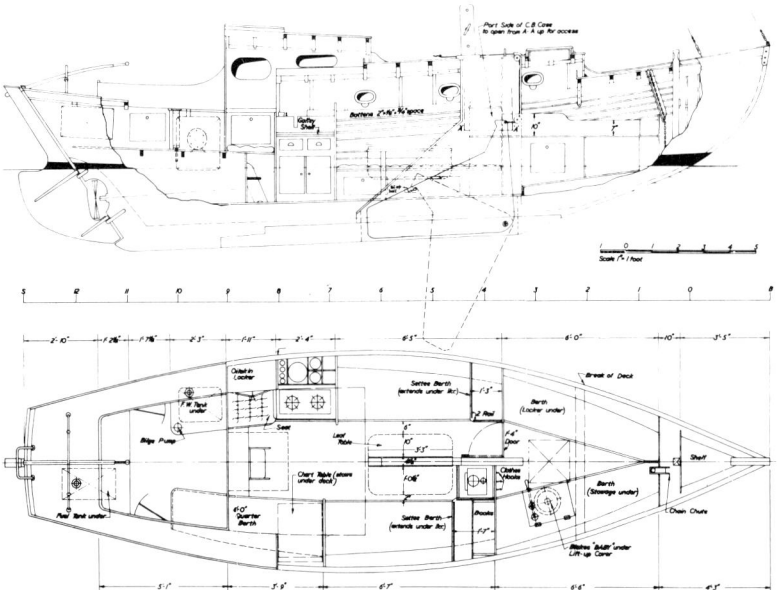

to pour a gallon or two of oil (old sump oil costs nothing) into the case while the yacht is afloat. The oil will, of course, float on top of the water. Let the yacht settle aground on the ebb, and as the water falls away the centreboard and the inside of the case will be well smothered, while hardly any oil escapes from the keel slot when the tide has gone. The marine parasites just hate the stuff, and incidentally the board will work more smoothly from then on.

As it turned out, only the first two yachts built to the *Barcarole* plans were fitted with the centreboard as designed. The idea of the advantages of deep bilge keels for shoal draft cruising yachts was already being accepted by sailing men, and subsequent boats of this class, not only at the Leigh-on-Sea yard but those home-built in Australia and South Africa, were bilge keelers. On occasions when one of the centreboarders could sail against a bilge keel version it seemed that there was little to choose between the two in general handling, quickness in stays, turning to windward in a smart breeze, or running with the wind free.

In fickle airs, the centreboarder with the long leading edge of its board when right down certainly had the advantage, for at very slow speeds the bilge keels with their comparatively short foward edge tended to stall and cause the yacht to make a good deal of leeway. On the other hand, owners said it was remarkable how the bilge keels acted as roll dampers when running before a sea on the quarter or right aft, and the boat's motion generally was steady and not so sick-making for members of the crew.

Putting a bilge keeler on the hard for a scrub, where she would sit firmly upright, was child's play compared with leaning a yacht against the scrubbing posts or quay; but this convenience is usually offset by the difficulty of getting at the hull between the bilge keels and the garboards. But while you wriggle in the space behind the bilge keel and toil upwards with scraper or brush with accompanying remarks, it is at least a comfort to know that the boat is unlikely to fall over on you. It is a sad record that many deep draft, sharp bottomed yachts and smacks alongside quays or posts have been known to fall over, and sometimes to crush the man at work under the bilge. Even legs lashed to the shrouds in the West Country fashion have been known to give way and let a deep boat topple onto her side. For those who do not want to win races there is much to be said for a good boat with bilge keels to steady her.

SOLANI

LOA	38.75 ft
LWL	30.00 ft
BEAM	10.50 ft
DRAFT	4.5 ft and 6.60 ft
DISPLACEMENT	10.38 ton
LEAD KEEL	3.15 ton
WKG SAIL AREA	720 sq ft
THAMES M'MT	14 ton

TOWARDS THE END of the Hitler War, the Committee of the Royal Naval Sailing Association was looking for designs which might appeal to members of Service yacht clubs for cruising and occasional racing, and possibly for the training of cadets at Dartmouth. Two types of yacht were to be considered, one a 20-foot WL V-bottom sloop for inshore cruising/racing; the other about 30-foot WL with limited draft for harbour and coastal cruising/racing.

Construction of the second class of yacht had to be simplified so that unit production could be utilised as far as practicable to reduce the rising costs in boat building to be expected in the post war period. The plans of *Solani*, with alternative sloop and ketch rig, were worked out with these requirements in mind, and through the efforts of Vice-Admiral Sir Geoffrey Blake, KCB, DSO, who was Commodore of the Association at the time, a scale model was made of the hull and put through a series of runs at the Hasler ship test tank. These trials gave apparently satisfactory results for a well balanced cruising yacht hull with ample sail carrying power.

In the event, although disappointed at the time that the designs submitted were eventually turned down, I think the Association's final

SOLANI

Malwen

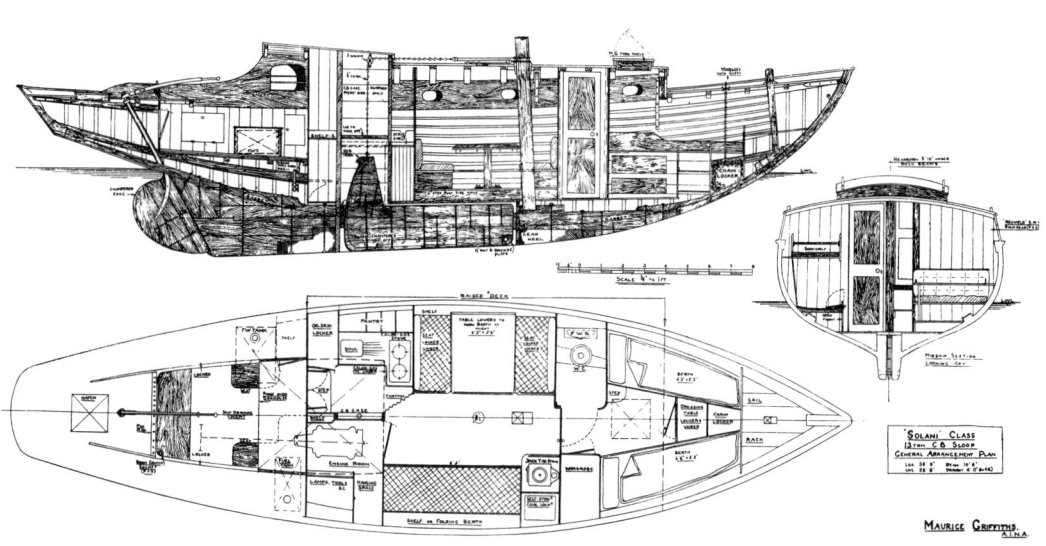

SOLANI

choice of a class of training yachts for the Navy of a more up-to-date racing type was a wise and perceptive one.

The first boat to be built after the war to my *Solani* design was the sloop rigged *Black Jack* which was constructed in 1947 by John I Thornycroft and Co at their Hampton-on-Thames yard. The centreboard was found unnecessary and was removed, while other modifications were carried out during the building. *Black Jack* has spent most of her sailing life in the Solent area. The second yacht of this design was a remarkable achievement by Stanley Hills, who built her in the garden of his house at West Mersea, Essex, in 1949. *Malwen*, stemhead sloop rigged and with her draft similarly increased to 5.5 feet with no centreboard, was noted for her great strength. The deck beams for the raised deck from the break at the foredeck to the cockpit were of steel angle section welded to form complete hoops which passed right round the hull, forming integral frames and floors.

The rest of the construction was in similar vein, for Mr Hills had seen what could happen to yachts or smacks which got on the concrete hard sands in the Thames Estuary, and was determined to have a really strong boat. The result of this is evident today — nearly forty years on — for the seams in *Malwen*'s smooth topsides still scarcely show and the hull shows no sign of ever working. Still based at West Mersea with her red topsides and varnished upper strake, *Malwen* spends each busy season with her present owner on club events and seamanship instruction.

Amongst other yachts which have been built to these plans we could note the ketch rigged *Sea Pie* (ex-*Zoraya*) which was built entirely of teak in 1949 by the Mazagon Shipyard in Bombay; *Musichana*, sloop rigged, constructed on a farm far inland from the East African coast in 1950, and *Sheelin*, stemhead cutter rigged, built by her owner and friends in 1951 at Freetown, Sierra Leone.

TINKA

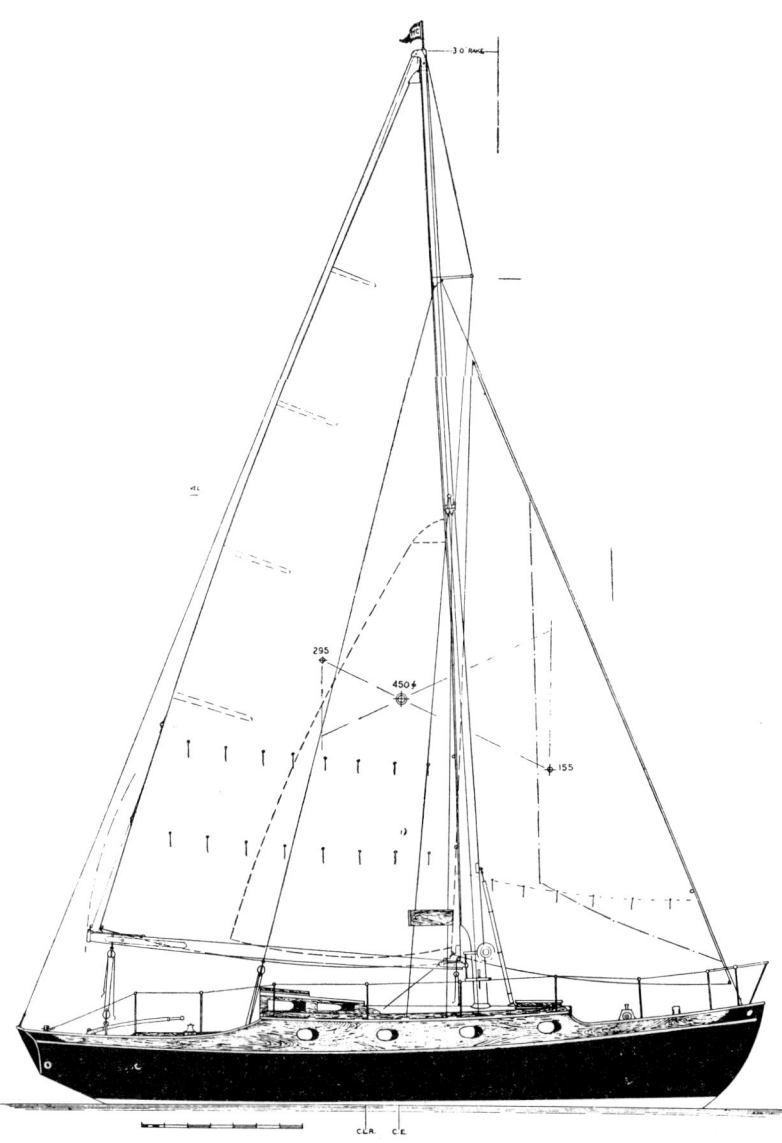

LOA	32.5ft
LWL	25.8ft
BEAM	10.0ft
DRAFT	5.0ft
DISPLACEMENT	6.85 tons
IRON KEEL	2.65 tons
WKG SAIL AREA	450 sq ft
THAMES M'MT	10 tons

A CLIENT WHO lived in Yorkshire asked for a design for a powerful, tough seaboat about 32 feet overall with roomy accommodation and draft limited to 5 feet as she would be kept on a half-tide mooring in Bridlington Harbour. Yachtsmen who base their craft here have to be dedicated sailors, for there are few other sheltered anchorages in either direction along this beautiful but inhospitable Yorkshire coast for an overnight stay. Sailing is mainly confined to a brief out-and-back foray on the tide, and handicap racing events claim most of the local activities.

TINKA

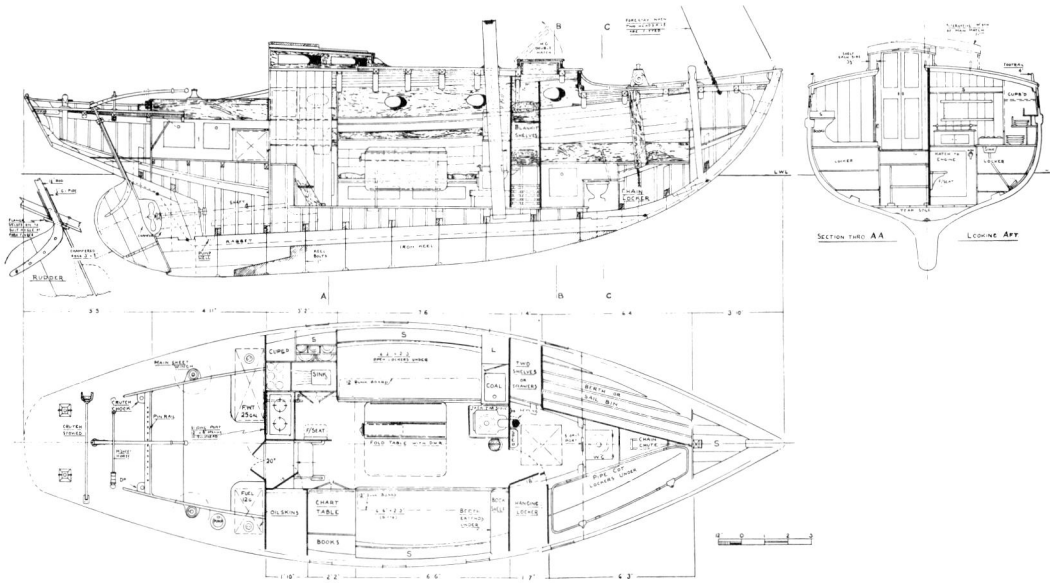

Tinka's design emerged as a result of these considerations, and she was built of first-class materials by Staniland and Co at Thorne near Doncaster, in 1951. She was a powerful boat with full-bodied sections which enabled her to sit upright in the soft mud of the harbour, and with her 10-foot beam and Griffiths' style raised midship deck layout there seemed an astonishing amount of room below. Between the 2-foot 3-inch wide settees in the cabin the sole was 3 feet 8 inches wide. The companionway was offset to starboard with a short fore-and-aft bulkhead allowing a snugly protected galley to port with fold-down seat for the cook.

A locker for oilskins opposite, together with a modest chart table (the owner did not plan ocean voyages) was balanced by a cosy coal stove against the forward bulkhead, with its zinc-lined fuel locker adjacent, which was welcome in almost any part of the season on the Yorkshire coast. Her varnished topsides and upper strake and short counter stern with arched transom gave *Tinka* a distinctive air amongst the varied collection of boats in the anchorage.

After a few seasons of day cruising and coastal essays the owner turned to some of the local handicap events, and after one or two near triumphs a stump bowsprit was added and an additional masthead stay fitted to carry bigger jibs. With these additions to the sail area *Tinka* justified her owner's faith by winning the Cruiser Class Points Cup in the 1961 season, and showed that she was not just a comfortable cruiser but could show a clean pair of heels when encouraged, a reet Yorkshire lass, by gum!

TINKA

TAMARIS

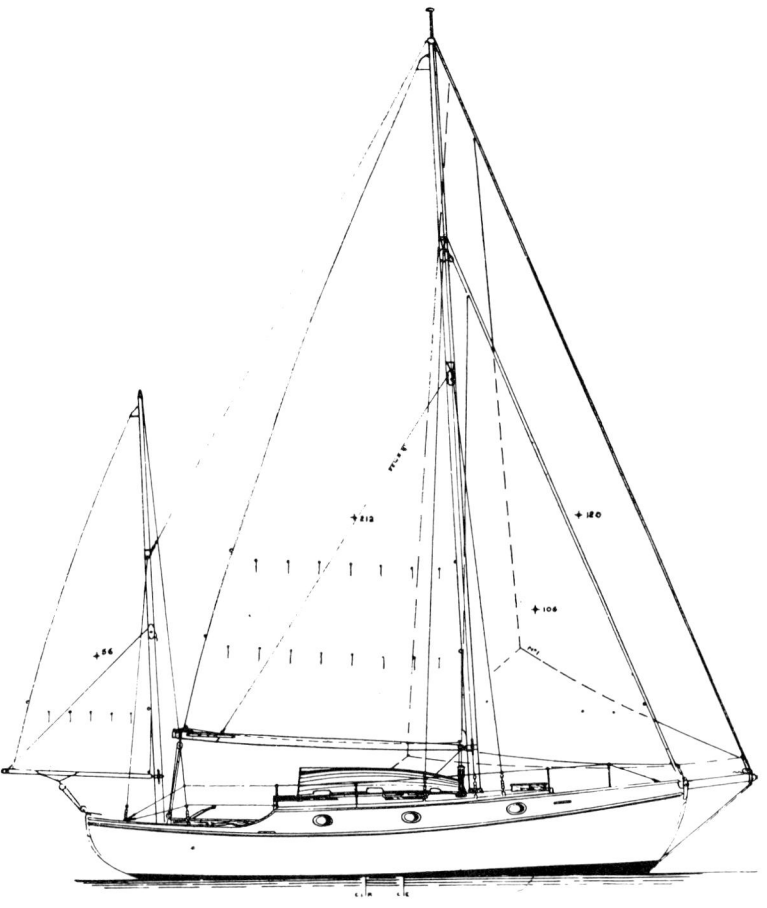

LOA	28.6ft
LWL	24.0ft
BEAM	8.3ft
DRAFT	4.3ft
DISPLACEMENT	5.10 tons
IRON KEEL	2.05 tons
WKG SAIL AREA	494 sq ft
THAMES M'MT	7 tons

FOR MANY YEARS I had been one of the admirers of the designs of Albert Strange, who was instrumental in introducing the canoe stern to the Humber Yawl Club while he was its Commodore. Albert Strange was art master at Scarborough College and was one of the most gifted of amateur yacht architects, and when he died in 1919 he left a legacy of designs of beautifully proportioned and graceful cruising yachts, the majority bearing versions of his shapely canoe sterns.

Lovely as all his boats were, however, Strange favoured only a modest beam, and with his finely drawn sections and soft turn to the bilge the amount of settee and leg room in the cabin of many of his smaller yachts did seem somewhat cramped by later standards. With the hindsight of the plagiarist I thought I would have a shot at a small yawl with a canoe stern like Strange's, but update her in certain features so as to gain the accommodation below decks which one expects in a small cruising boat today, and enable her to carry a dinghy on deck.

TARMARIS

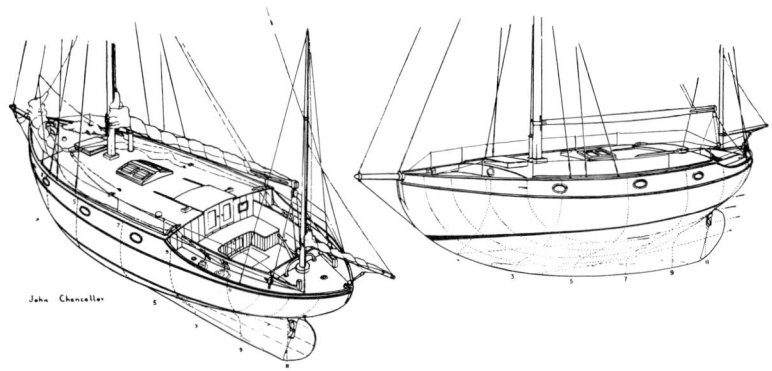

In the 40-foot *Juliana* (page 57) I had already produced a boat with a canoe stern which seemed to blend with the rest of the ship, and when a friend agreed that if we both liked the new design he would have a sister ship built in the same yard at the same time. I got down to the drawing board. Thereupon, the little *Tamaris* took shape in Johnson and Jago's yard at Leigh-on-Sea, with my friend's *Safari* following to the same plans alongside.

With less draft than a Strange boat the hull was given fuller sections, so that there was a width of 2 feet 9 inches between the settee berths. From the break of deck at the foredeck to the cockpit the main deck was raised flush, with a skylight over the cabin table and a low main hatch. A raised mainhatch was avoided reluctantly so that an 8-foot pram could be carried bottom up between hatch and mainmast. In the self-draining cockpit the tiller came up through a slot in the after bulkhead, with the mizzen mast stepped on the deck above. This made the yacht technically a ketch, but she was always referred to as a yawl, and the arrangement enabled a useful size of mizzen, well stayed, to be fitted.

Planking of both boats was ⅞ inch West African mahogany on English oak steamed timbers 1¼ inch by 1 inch at 6 inch spacing. The stern was, I think, a success and helped to make them pretty little things indeed, but I confess I was shaken by the cost of framing and shaping this canoe stern compared with that for a normal transom, for its curves required eight sawn oak frames aside, 2 inches by 2¼ inches each of a different section. The forehatch and the opening skylight were of the double-coaming pattern I introduced some 50 years ago, and which has generally proved leakproof at sea on the yachts fitted with it.

The yawl rig with its jib and staysail hanked to their stays, the jib-cut mainsail not laced to the boom, and the useful mizzen proved a great success in practice. The mizzen of 56 square feet was just large enough to turn to windward with either staysail or jib — although slower in stays — while the little boat would do anything asked for under her mainsail

TARMARIS

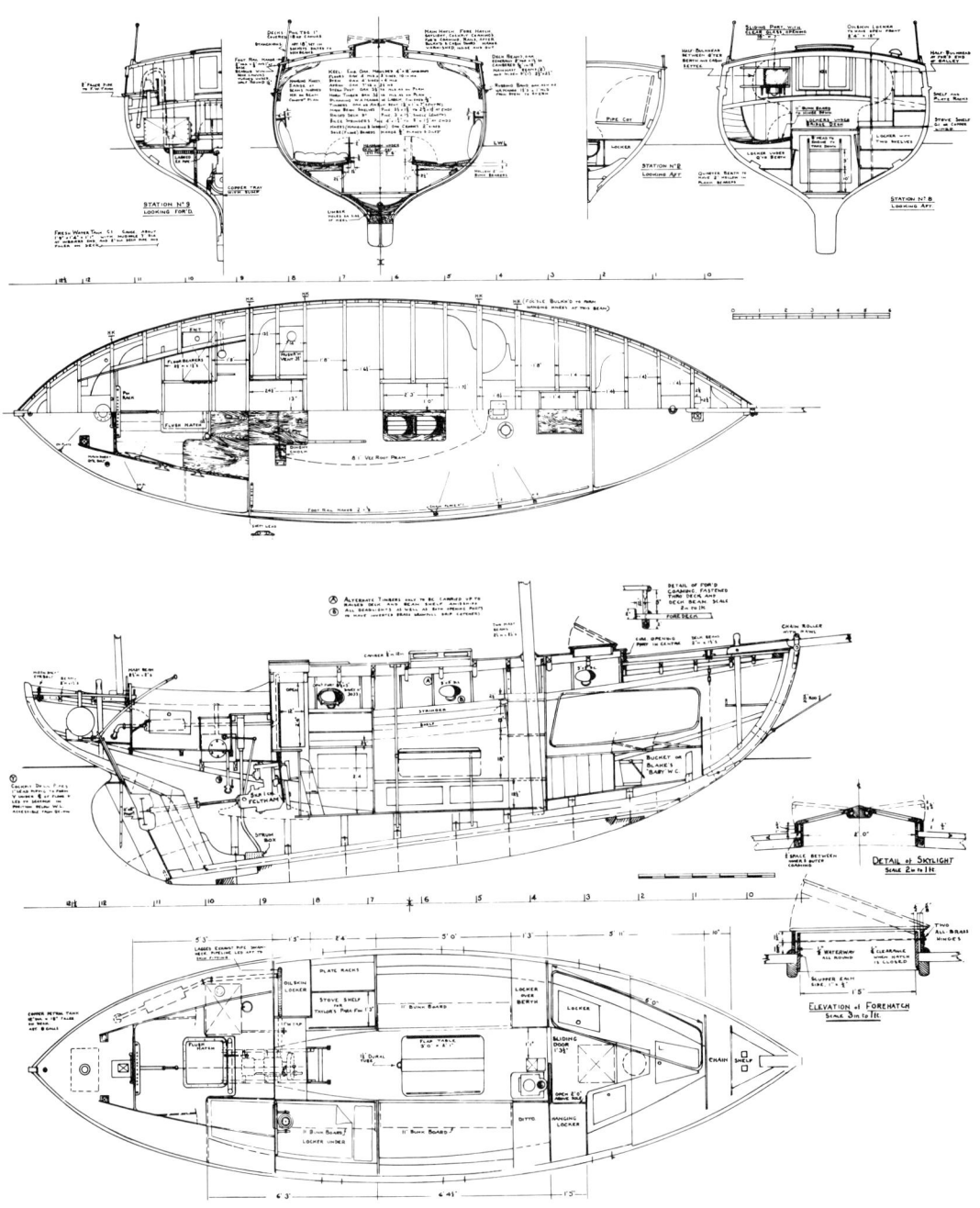

(full or reefed) alone. *Tamaris*, in fact, turned out a delightful little ship with no particular vices, although just to show how impossible it is to build two wooden vessels exactly alike in every particular, whereas *Tamaris* was light on the helm under most sailing conditions, her sistership *Safari*, built in the same shed by the same hands, always carried a fair amount of weather helm. No one could explain why this was and it is a phenomenon to be met amongst boats of all kinds which are considered identical. It is well known in the engineering world where machines which have been built to identical patterns can each show their own variations in behaviour, some good and well behaved, similar ones becoming rogues. Sod's Law, they tell me.

Other boats later followed to this design, including *Veterata*, built at Whitstable by Anderson, Rigden and Perkins, a specially good specimen with a lead keel and other refinements; *Triton* III built under Swiss ownership for sailing on Lake Lucerne, and one or two others which were built in Australia.

JEANNE D'ARC

LOA	39.5ft
LWL	32.0ft
BEAM	9.8ft
DRAFT	6.5ft
DISPLACEMENT	10.24 tons
IRON KEEL	4.85 tons
WKG SAIL AREA	675 sq ft
THAMES M'MT	14 tons

A FEW YEARS before the Hitler war I was asked to design as an experiment a wishbone ketch sail plan for a 32-foot ex-Porthleven lugger, *Restless of Plyn*, owned by Lady Browning (Daphne du Maurier, the novelist). The combination of the heavy hull of the deep-bodied Cornish fisherman and this type of rig was not altogether the best one, for although the wishbone rig had many points in its favour in ease of handling, quick sail reduction in squally weather, and close-windedness without any of the sails being backwinded, it was more suited to a light weight easily driven hull.

In 1951, General Sir Fredk. Browning asked me to design for the family a yacht more suited to this divided rig. The old *Restless* had gone to pieces on the beach during the war, but her spars and fittings and sails had survived, and much of the gear could be used aboard the new ship. With the owner's approval the design of *Jeanne d'Arc* took the form of an enlarged version of the 24-foot WL canoe yawl *Tamaris*, but with a finer entry in the bow and a deeper keel having a straight underside to keep the yacht level when legged up on the beach in West Country fashion.

The yacht was strongly built at Hunkin's yard, Polruan-by-Fowey, using locally felled oak for keel, deadwoods, floors, frames and deck beams. Planking was best West African mahogany, while the mainmast was a solid pole which came from nearby Restormal Woods. The owners were keen to avoid the persistent deck leaks which had plagued them aboard the old *Restless*, and the new yacht's main deck was accordingly raised amidships from the foredeck to the break at the cockpit, and carried flush across the beam in the same manner as that adopted for *Ionia*, *Solani*, *Tinka* and *Tamaris*. The 1¼-inch tongue and groove pine decks were covered overall with sheets of ¼-inch Presdwood edge-glued together, thereby virtually forming a single sheet from which no signs of leaks were said to appear for many years.

With her fine lined hull and, for a West Country boat, modest displacement, *Jeanne d'Arc* proved particularly handy under almost all combinations of sails in her wishbone rig. Like her smaller relative, *Tamaris*, she would steer herself on most points of sailing, and when punching to windward in a fresh Channel breeze she usually kept her decks free from anything but spray.

A near-sister ship to this design, *Quintila*, was built in 1955 by the Minnow Yacht Co at Paignton to 100 A1 Class under Lloyd's survey. Her overall measurements were 40.0 feet on deck, 32.2 feet WL, 10.0 feet beam and 6.4 feet draft. The wishbone rig was identical to that of *Jeanne d'Arc* with a working sail area of 675 square feet. Whereas General Browning's yachts sported a dark blue hull with a substantial varnished mahogany rubbing strake at deck level, *Quintila* (as the accompanying photograph shows) was given white topsides without any rubbing strake.

JEANNE D'ARC

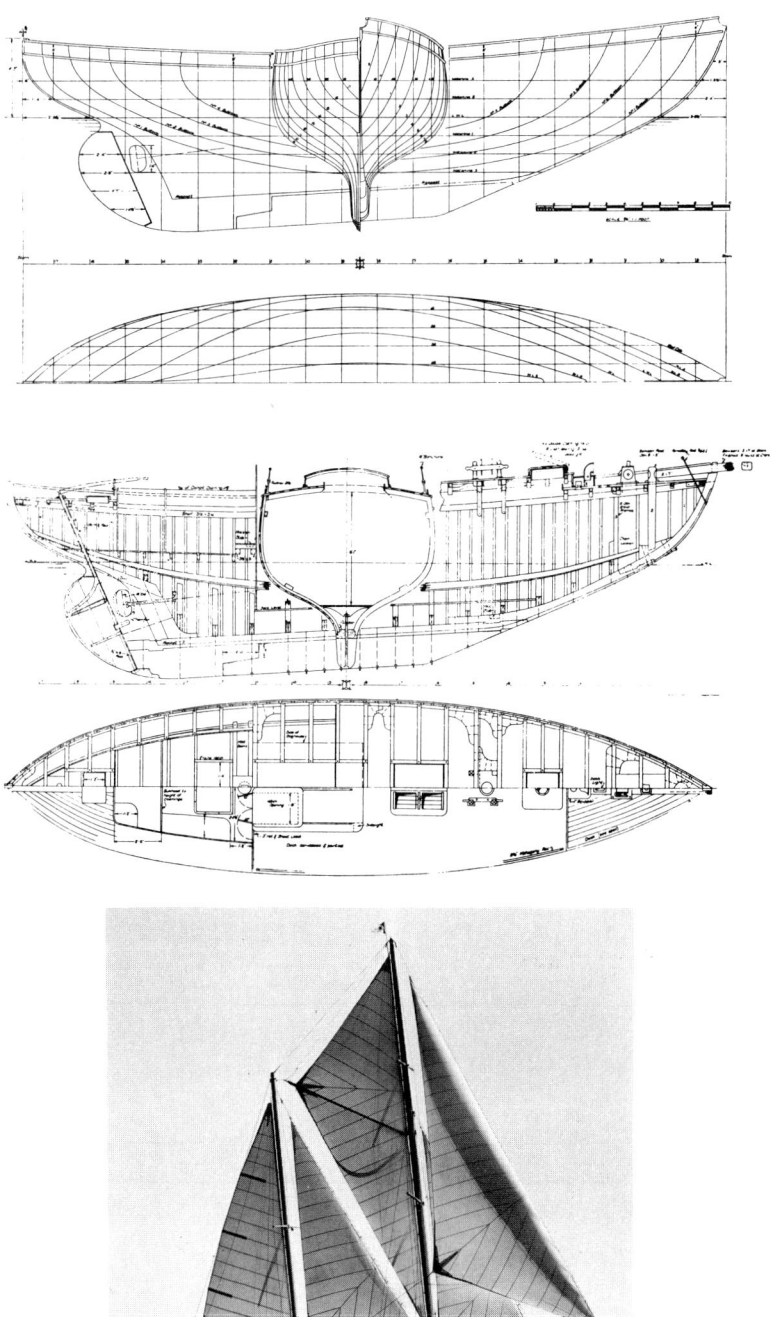

Quintila

KISMET

LOA	38.5ft
LWL	28.4ft
BEAM	11.0ft
DRAFT	4.0ft and 9.0ft
DISPLACEMENT	9.36 tons
LEAD KEEL	3.75 tons
WKG SAIL AREA	658 sq ft
WITH GENOA	919 sq ft
THAMES M'MT	17 tons

DURING THE 1950s, the racing records of a number of American shallow draft centreboard yachts shook the complacency of many British yachtsmen who shared traditional notions of yacht design by demonstrating the speed and capabilities possible with well designed shallow bodied yachts. It started when American yachtsman Carleton Mitchell won the transatlantic race to Plymouth in 1952 with his 58-foot yawl *Caribbee*, a Phil Rhodes-designed centreboarder, and continued with other successes against English yachts in their home waters. Then the lovely *Carina*, a 53-foot centreboard yawl, also a Rhodes design, first won the 1955 race from Newport, Rhode Island, to Sweden and followed this by winning boat for boat in Class II the Fastnet race that same season.

KISMET

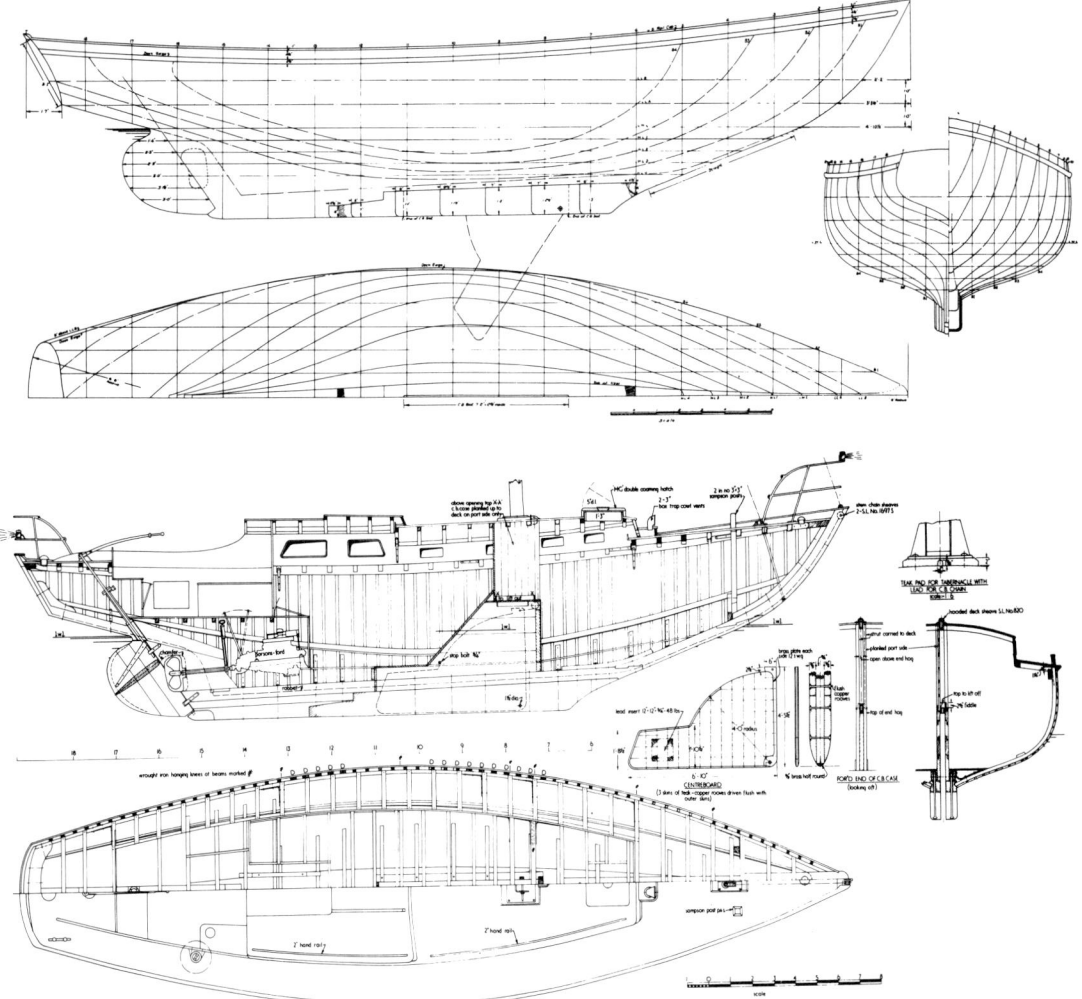

On parting with his *Caribee*, Carleton Mitchell had a 39-foot centreboard yawl designed this time by Olin Stephens, and what became known as the *Finisterre* type was born. From the first, *Finisterre* proved a remarkable boat. On a waterline of 27 feet 6 inches she had 11 feet 3 inches beam with under 4 feet draft with the metal plate raised, and 7 feet 7 inches with it fully down, and out of 33 races in which she sailed against some of the best CCA class yachts she gained 26 firsts, 2 seconds and 3 third places. It was not all won through a favourable handicap or low rating; *Finisterre* sailed her races boat for boat and beat them. It seemed that American demonstrations in fast shallow draft yachts might influence design thought in this country.

Following these events the experienced owner of a Griffiths-designed 40-foot ketch with something over 6 feet 6 inches draft, who had wit-

KISMET

nessed both *Caribbee* and *Carina* outsail other yachts in their class in Solent waters, decided to replace his deep-keeler with a centreboarder of roughly the same tonnage. Rather than build to an American design, however, he asked me to produce my own version of a 38-foot centreboarder with a draft of less than 4 feet, a seakindly motion, a good turn of speed, and roomy accommodation for a family to explore the upper reaches of West Country rivers and harbours along the Brittany coast.

The design, reproduced here, aimed at a powerful sail-carrying hull with a comparatively high potential speed when heeled 15 degrees or so. With her firm sections and ample beam her angle of heel when sailing normally would allow glasses to stay on the cabin table without gimballs, and the spaciousness below decks would be that of a rather larger boat. The layout in fact followed closely that of the owner's 40-foot ketch, but with the benefit of 18in more beam, and placed the galley, pantry and the extra hand's own toilet forward of the mast. Comfort in the saloon was gained by two settee berths 6 feet 6 inches long and alcoves at the backs for books, radio and oddments. At the after end a hinged chart table over a quarter berth with seat was balanced with, to port, a toilet compartment large enough for a shower and cupboard for wet clothes.

Headroom under coachroof beams was 6 feet 2 inches throughout with extra inside the main hatch. A slow combustion cabin stove against the forward bulkhead would take care of comfort in the driving mists met with in West Country waters.

Before the ketch could be sold and an order placed for the new centre-

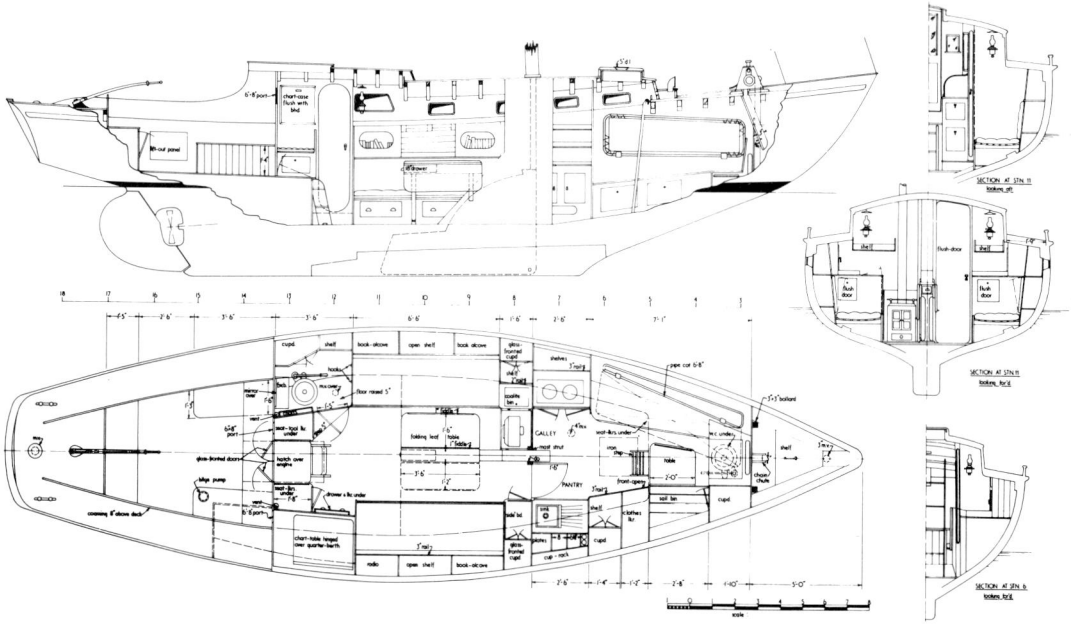

boarder with a local yard, tragically the owner died and the design was put on one side. A few years later an enquiry was received from a syndicate in Western Australia for a design of very similar characteristics, again with shallow estuaries and lagoons in the Pacific in the offing, and so *Kismet* took shape down under.

Except for some modifications to the interior layout to suit the new owners' requirements and local conditions, the hull lines, rig and rigging details were unchanged, and the yacht was sturdily built using the excellent boatbuilding timbers obtained locally. The centreboard was built up with three thicknesses of hardwood ⅝ inches on the outside and ¾ inch inside with a 12 inch by 12 inch slab of lead weighing 48 pounds inserted to take the board down with negative buoyancy. The forward part of the case came up above the waterline with lift-off cover, while the upper part extended to the deck as a support for the mast. The arrangement is clearly shown in the construction drawing reproduced.

That is all nearly 30 years ago, and although I had news of the yacht with photographs from her owners, with enthusiastic reports on her sailing ability and behaviour in a seaway, I have not heard of *Kismet*'s whereabouts now for many years.

LONE GULL II

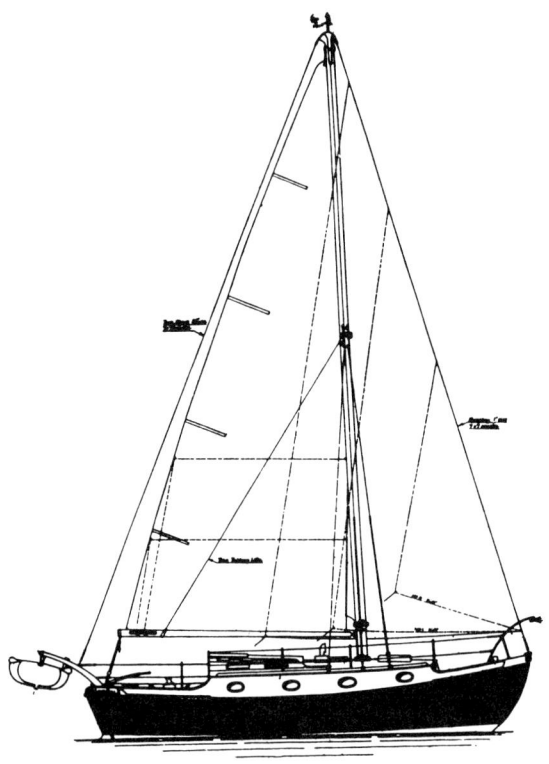

LOA	28.0 ft
LWL	24.0 ft
BEAM	9.0 ft
DRAFT	3.3 ft
DISPLACEMENT	5.71 tons
IRON KEEL	1.89 tons
WKG SAIL AREA	398 sq ft
THAMES M'MT	8 tons

BY 1960, a large number of designs of small yachts had appeared on the scene with twin ballast keels or with a central iron keel and twin bilge keels. Robert Tucker's popular *Silhouettes* were being produced in quantity together with others of his bilge keel designs, while since 1957 the *Yachting Monthly* had been supplying large numbers of plans for the home builder for the *Eventide*, 24-foot and 26-foot versions, and had now launched the *Waterwitch* 30, all chine boats with a central iron keel and steel bilge keel plates.

Sailing men were becoming acclimatised to the notion of having twin keels on a cruising boat, and the convenience they offered the family in squatting upright on a beach for bathing and picnics, or for attention to some underwater part of the hull, made a decided appeal to the owner not racing minded. The value of being able to float in three and a half feet of water at many yacht harbours where silting of mud was steadily reducing the number of berths that could float yachts of, say, 6-foot draft, was becoming recognised as a practical consideration. The difference between 3½ feet and 6 feet might not seem much when there is so much water in the rivers and channels around our coasts, but in a crowded yacht marina or at the upper reaches of many a creek, those two feet or more can make all the difference between a comfortable berth and a crowded and restless one.

LONE GULL II

Through pressure of work I had been without a boat of my own for several years, but began working on the plans of a 28-footer so as to find out at first hand just what advantages — and disadvantages — one could reap from bilge keels. Recalling what a pleasing type of boat my prewar *Lone Gull* I had been, I aimed at producing an updated model on generally similar lines, but smaller in view of the immense increase in building costs. The new boat was to have a substantial iron keel on the centreline to ensure a return from a knockdown and, in place of the centreboard, twin bilge keels for sand squatting upright. My wife and I were living at Haslemere in Surrey at the time, from where I was able to commute daily to the *Yachting Monthly* offices, and the order for *Lone Gull* II was accordingly placed with Harry Feltham's yard in Old Portsmouth.

The large coachroof of *Lone Gull* I with its leak-prone deck joints was avoided this time by the raised midship deck construction I had come to adopt in many other designs. It gave us standing headroom through into the fo'cs'le and a few inches more under the main hatchway. The layout plan below was uninspired but a well tried and practical one. A lobby with toilet and clothes hanging locker opposite separated the two-berth fo'cs'le from the cabin with its usual settee berths and side lockers.

These settees were made up in the style I have introduced in many boats: instead of the bottom planks being flat and airless, they are planked with fore and aft battens with ¼ inch airspaces between them and given a 1½ inch hollow athwartships. Especially if the berth mattresses are not thick and springy this slight hollow adds much to one's comfort at night. The galley I generally try to arrange to port in small yachts, because if you have to get a meal while hove-to in boisterous weather, you are wise always to lie-in on the starboard tack (with the wind on the starboard bow) in which position you will have right of way over other vessels approaching on the port tack or with wind free. But do not take it all for granted, for these days it pays to take an occasional peep out of the hatch for the odd big ship blundering along on automatic pilot without

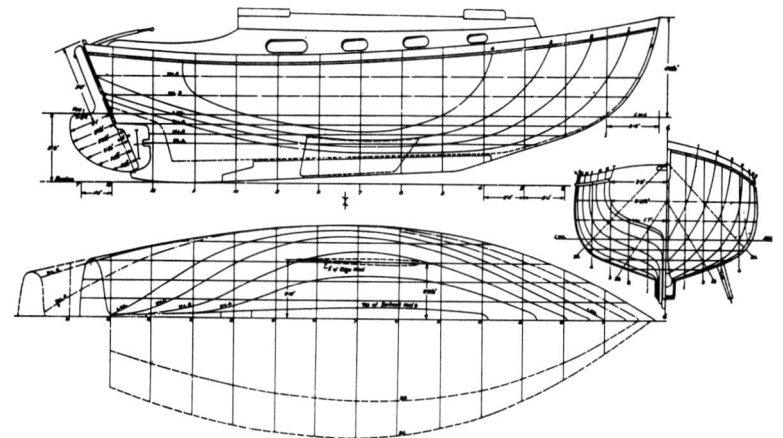

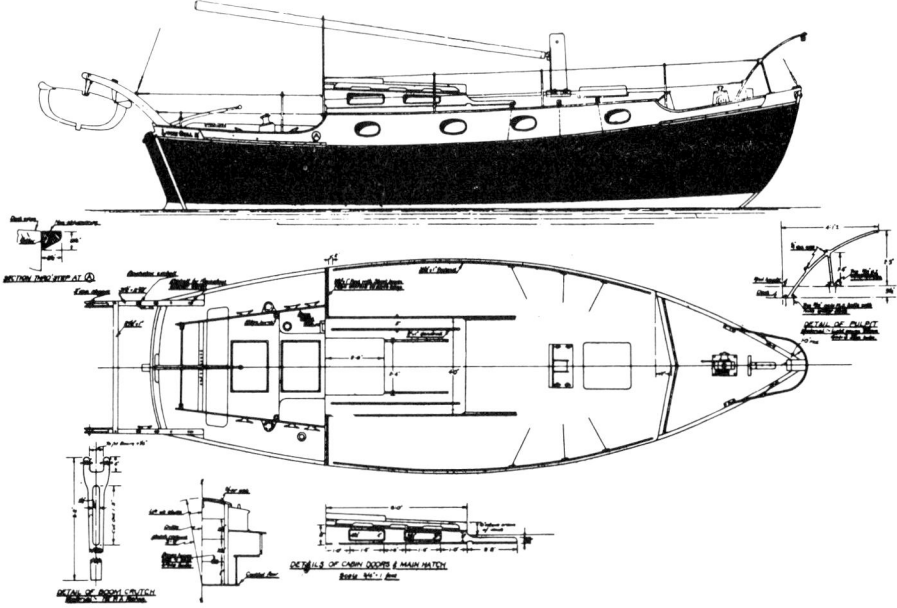

a soul visible on board; or the fast and expensive yacht on a collision course whose owner has not yet learnt the implications of another yacht being on starboard tack. It does happen all too often.

The ship's boat, a lightweight flattie pram from Souters at Cowes, was carried athwart the transom on oak horns (stern davits) in Baltic fashion. Except when lying alongside other yachts on a trot we found this a very convenient way of keeping the dinghy quiet all night or at sea. But I think *Lone Gull* II was about the minimum size of yacht to carry her dinghy in this way.

From our moorings at Hardway in Portsmouth Harbour, Marjorie and I enjoyed two very happy seasons exploring Solent waters, and found *Lone Gull* II's shallow draft and ability to perch upright on sand and mud highly convenient when we tried poking our way into Bembridge and the upper reaches of Chichester and Langstone harbours, the Beaulieu river, Newtown, Keyhaven and the channels of Poole Harbour and up the river as far as Wareham bridge.

In the Mate's opinion all these charming places and the wide Solent itself were indisputably more attractive and colourful than any of the East Coast rivers and creeks where I had introduced her to sailing after the war. Certainly I should not care to argue otherwise, for on bright days of sun, wind and cloud contrasts the Solent and both its shores can offer breathtaking varieties of colour which are all too rare on the waters of the Thames Estuary, and appeal strongly to my wife as an artist.

Lone Gull II turned out a happy combination of a docile ship which was tough enough to face up to strong winds without lying on her side. The

LONE GULL II

firm bilges took care of that, apart from the weight in her iron keel, and about 15 degrees of heel was her normal angle in any good sailing breeze. It was very comfortable sailing.

The bilge keels proved very effective as roll dampers. When running before a steep sea aft or on either quarter she would every now and then take a lurch to leeward, roll back and then continue on hardly rolling, as though on rails: there was never any of that sick-making rhythmic rolling so often met in deep keel yachts with slack bilges. For my wife, who is prone to seasickness, *Lone Gull* II was a special boat, for Marjorie never once was sick on board, despite some rough passages we made together in and out of the Solent waters.

At one time we had plans to move home to Lymington, when I was due to retire from the *Yachting Monthly* in a few years' time, so as to carry on my yacht design work and book writing while Marjorie would have her own studio. But other business intervened, reluctantly we had to part with *Lone Gull* — she went to a keen young single-handed sailorman who used her well — and moved our home back to the East Coast. At any rate we had fond memories of Solent sailing with a bilge keeler just before the whole area with its rivers and harbours was to become almost choked with yachts and money.

LONE GULL II

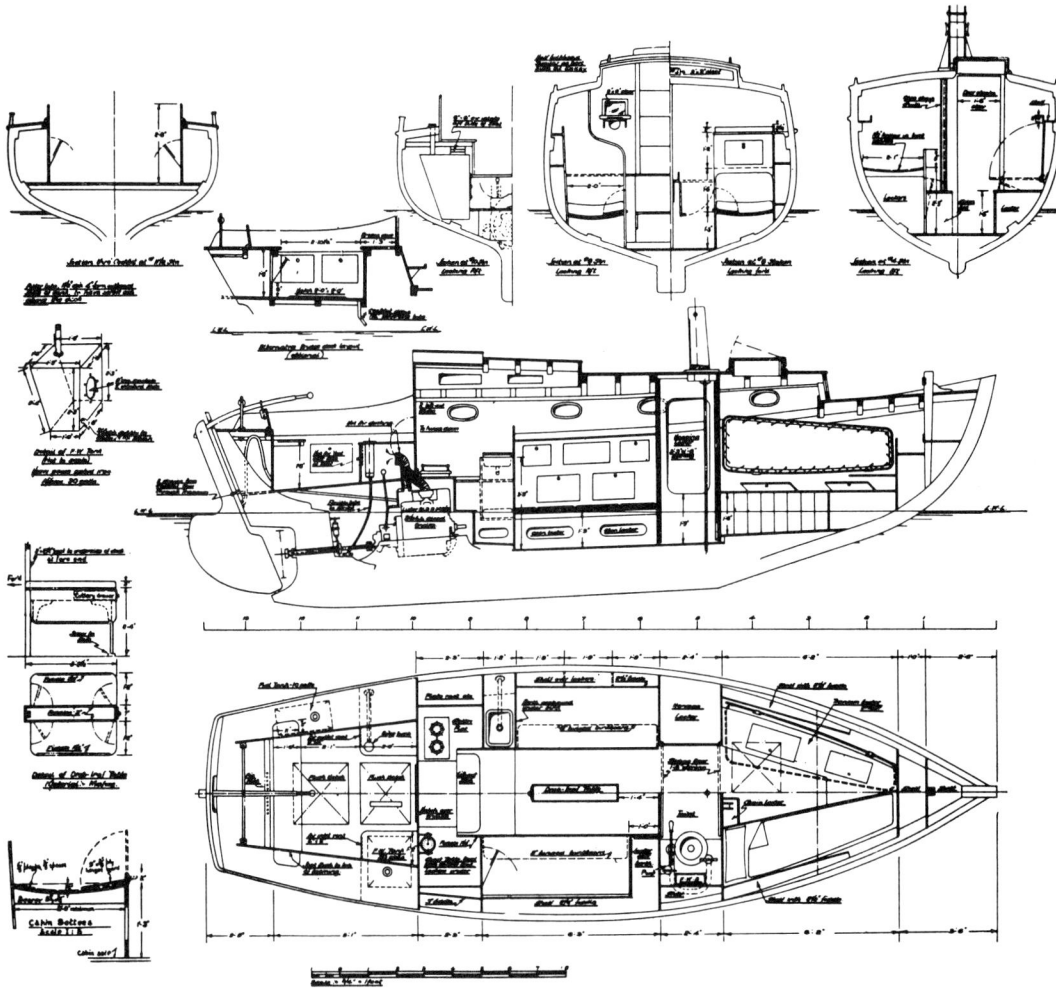

Several boats have since been built to this design and have been greatly liked by their owners for their dryness in a chop, their seakindly behaviour in strong weather, and their uncanny habit of steering themselves with sails and tiller adjusted with the wind anywhere from the bow to either quarter. Some have been owner-built in Australia, while one was constructed in the shipyard at Suva, Fiji, for the harbour master and his wife who managed to explore many lagoons in the surrounding islands inaccessible to deeper draft yachts. Others of the class have appeared in moulded resinglass from Brue Yachts, Blakes Boatyard, Highbridge, Somerset.

On the whole I would say the *Lone Gull* II class are sensible, all round shallow draft cruising boats for those who do not have a racing bug gnawing at them, and who appreciate a boat that knows how to look after herself and her crew.

TIDEWATER

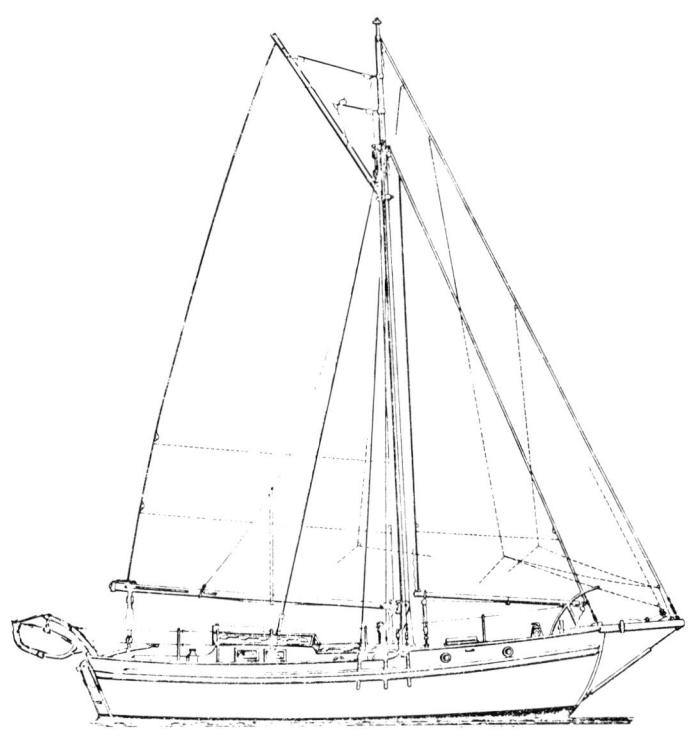

LOA	30.0ft
LWL	26.2ft
BEAM	9.5ft
DRAFT	3.4ft
DISPLACEMENT	6.6 tons
BALLAST KEEL	2.1 tons
WKG SAIL AREA	514 sq ft
THAMES M'MT	10 tons

FOLLOWING THE advent of the *Lone Gull* II type, there appeared to be a demand for something of a similar type but a size bigger which was of simple, uncomplicated construction so that it could be built in back yards or by native craftsmen used only to building fishing boats. Bearing these possibilities in mind I designed a plain traditional hull which could be framed either with steam-bent timbers like a yacht, or by sawn frames like a fisherman.

With a short overhang forward and a moderately raked transom stern the lines naturally followed closely those of *Lone Gull* II, but the additional length of 2 feet and a beam of 9.5 feet gave *Tidewater* an immensely roomy and powerful hull for a 30-footer. The original deck plan as drawn followed that of the 28-footer's with the raised deck amidships with a break at the foredeck, carried far enough forward of the mast to contain the double-coaming forehatch. The short foredeck was therefore unencumbered by a hatch, while the upper strake and railcap was carried forward to the bow to from a 6-inch protective footrail.

The depth of this larger hull, however, allowed just enough height above the cabin settees to sit upright under normal side decks, and as several builders asked for this alternative, a new deck layout was drawn up with a raised foredeck reaching aft to the mast (and giving full headroom in a fore-cabin), thence from a break side decks 2 feet in width ran to the stern with a coachroof ending in a low doghouse or main hatch. This became the standard deck arrangement for the *Tidewater* class, and is illustrated in the accompanying drawings.

Some 40 boats of this design have been built since the 1960s, in diverse places such as Essex, Kent, Hampshire, North Devon and Ireland; and overseas in boat yards or backyards in Australia, Tasmania, New Zealand, Uganda, Nigeria, Ghana, South Africa, Trinidad and California. Some have been hammered together on the beach in palm fringed yards and framed in native style with sawn frames throughout and a variety of timbers hardly known back in Britain. Others have been built with strip edge-nailed and glued planking, while one, constructed by her owner and a shipwright friend in Kent had a clinker built hull. With the plank lands accentuating the sheer of the hull and the mahogany topsides and upper strake varnished, this was an outstandingly pretty version.

The rigs adopted by *Tidewater* owners have ranged from the conventional stemhead Bermuda sloop (with a tendancy to carry a fair amount of weather helm) and Bermuda cutter with short plank bowsprit (giving more sail area in its headsails and a nice balance on the helm) to one or two gaff cutter rigs which suited the hull well. Individual tastes have been revealed in one boat (*Delphis* from Tasmania) which carried a wishbone schooner rig, and in a bowsprit cutter with jib and forestays'l and a Chinese junk mainsail, from South Africa, which made the crossing to the West Indies. I believe all these boats had the bilge keels fitted as on the plans, although with the long ballast keel these bilge keels are optional and intended to suit local requirements.

To meet various requests which were received for a ferrocement version for overseas backyard building, I produced the *Blue Water* design. To enable the pipeframes to be bent round the hull the garboards were rounded into the keel sides, and the trough keel deepened to take the weight of cemented-in iron scrap ballast. The result was a draft increased to 4 feet 9 inches with curved garboards and, of course, an increased

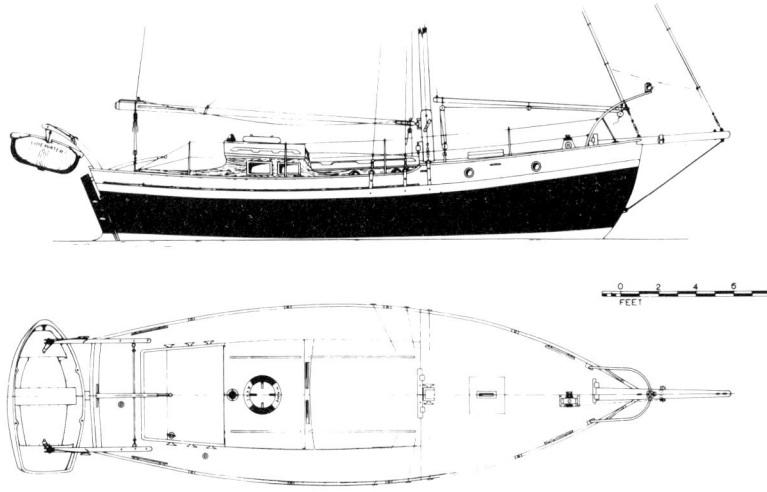

displacement, but with all other features of deck layout, accommodation plan and choice of rig following the wooden boat. The ferro *Blue Water* class, as expected, were built mainly in Australia, New Zealand and in Africa, where their construction suited the climate.

On the whole the *Tidewater* and *Blue Water* designs turned out successful boats, proving very docile to handle (especially those with short bowsprits) either singlehanded or with a short crew. They were seakindly, dry and easy in their movements in a seaway, and with the same useful faculty of the 28-foot *Lone Gull* II class of being able to keep a straight course with the tiller pegged or slip-hitch held with the wind anywhere between the bow and the quarter. Some have proved comfortable homes for their owners and mates, and their ability to work their way into shallow creeks and lagoons, or to settle upright on a beach has also proved a welcome feature for a family boat.

With the long keel from forefoot to the rudder heel and short overhangs, a firm turn to the bilges and general form of construction, the *Tidewater*

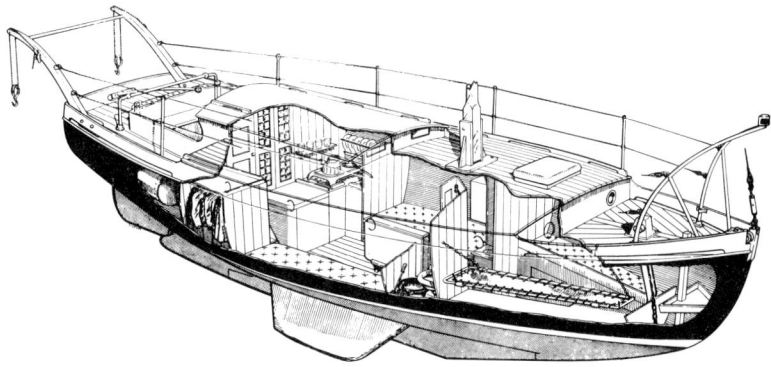

boats are as wholly traditional and as old fashioned as a brass oil lamp. It is, however, a type which has come through many generations of use in yachts and amongst the fishing fleets, and like all their predecessors, yachts of this kind appear lethargic in their movements. They will take their time in coming about from one tack to another, for they cannot be spun round in stays like a sailing dinghy or any of today's fin-keel-spade-rudder racers.

Contemporary yachtsmen who have been brought up only in these agile plastic fin keelers face problems when handling for the first time a traditional long keel yacht like a *Tidewater*. 'She just won't go about,' they exclaim in disgust. 'The bitch misses stays more often than not, however hard I push the helm down.'

The age old art of sailing a boat like that around into the wind with only gently increasing helm, then keeping the staysail aback — not a second too long — until her head is almost onto the other tack, has to be learnt with practice. Once learnt it becomes second nature to work the long keeler with certainty — like any old time smack tacking into a harbour — into any narrow creek or crowded anchorage.

'But she won't go to wind'ard, either,' objects the racing helmsman, 'however hard I pin her in'. That is another thing in which the old timer needs understanding. There are numerous action photographs in yachting magazines and in the daily press in summer showing racing yachts slicing along close-hauled with the crew perched along the weather rail like a row of starlings, while above the helmsman at his giant wheel the end of the mainboom looks almost over the very centreline of the deck. In the class racing machines with their lightweight hulls and astonishing performance that is precisely how the mainsail needs to be pinned in when on a wind.

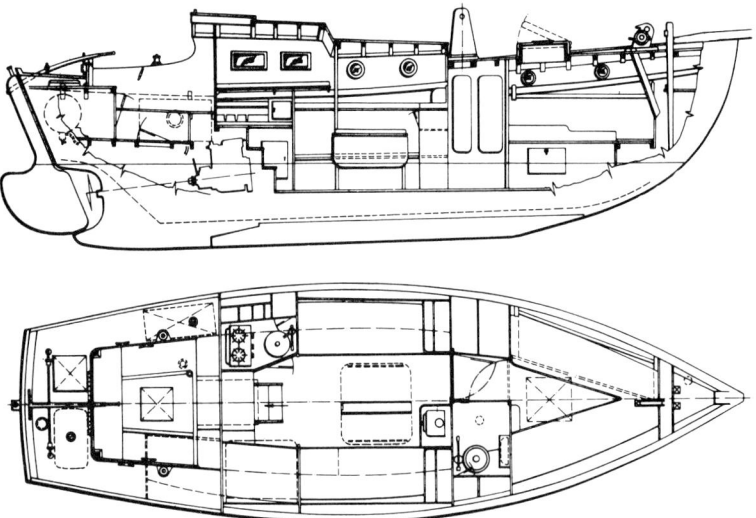

But if you try to emulate this strapped-in mainsheet aboard a traditional cruising yacht of any kind she will go dead on you, will show a mulish reluctance to slicing away to windward, and will probably be making excessive leeway, disheartening to everyone on board. Every yacht has her own characteristics, even amongst a class of similar boats, but for an average traditional cruising type, whether deep draft or shallow, it is usually found that when close-hauled on the wind boats of this kind like the end of the main boom hauled in until it is just over the lee coaming of the cockpit.

Only by much trial and error (sailing in company with other yachts helps) and bearing in mind the flatness or fullness in the cut of the mainsail, will the boat show you what suits her best when on a wind. And the best angle for the headsail sheets is always worth experimenting with when underway. In fresh winds hard in on the winches, but in light weather an inch or two eased so as to allow the headsails a little more flow without fluttering, is a golden rule towards getting a boat through the water.

GOOD HOPE

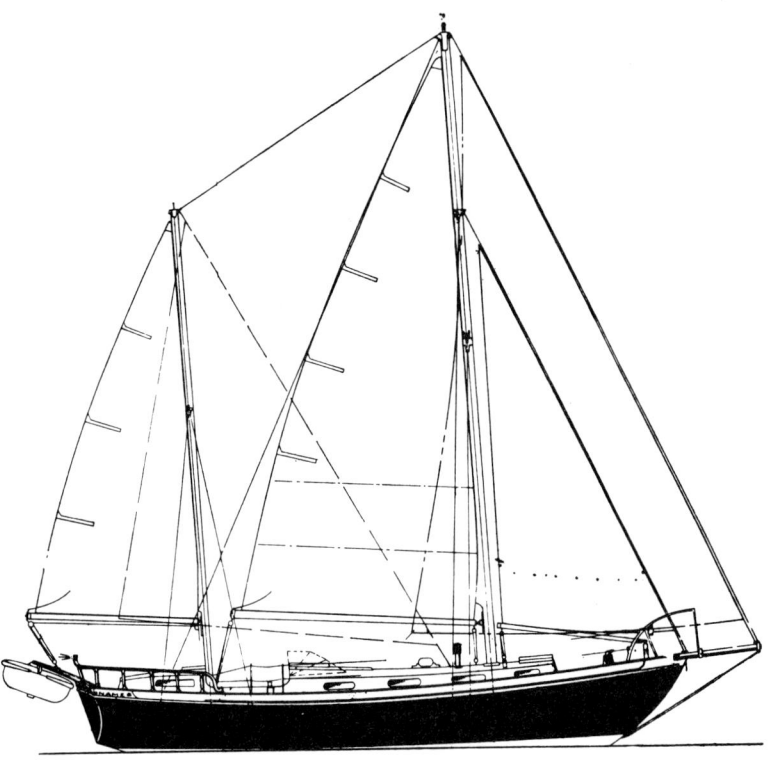

Loa	38.5ft
Lwl	30.5ft
Beam	11.0ft
Draft	4.3ft
Displacement	10.67 tons
Iron keel	4.0 tons
Wkg sail area	732 sq ft
Thames m'mt	16 tons

MY AGE WAS nearing 65 and I was looking forward to retiring from the *Yachting Monthly*, giving up the daily commuters' train to the London office, and settling to a quieter life and more writing at home. A doctor friend with a practice in Aldeburgh, however, had other ideas; he had decided to fulfil half a lifetime's ambition to have a comfortable yacht built for his growing family, and was determined that it must be a Griffiths' design.

The more I hedged the greater the persuasion John Stevens put on me, with the result that as soon as I had finished in London, dried the tears and settled at home, plans of *Good Hope* began to take shape on my drawing board. The requirements were clear, although fairly elaborate: the ship was to be capable of taking for weekends and coastal cruises John's family of five young children with three adults, and accompanied by the family's two Labrador tailwaggers who refused to be left behind. The limit of draught was set at not over 4 feet 6 inches with the continental inland waterways in mind when more leisure time became available. There was to be no centreboard, while fresh water and fuel capacity was set at about 95 gallons each.

So that the children could pull their weight in setting and trimming the sails, Bermuda ketch rig was chosen with a moderate sail area, even the mainsail being within the capacity of 10- and 12-year-olds to manage together. John had already crossed the Atlantic as the seaman-surgeon with Alan Villiers aboard the replica *Mayflower* 10 years before in 1957, and had acquired a liking for plain simple gear and rigging (with no elaborate and costly winches and fittings) which could all be worked by a lightweight crew.

An overriding consideration was that the all-in cost must not exceed a modest figure (which seen now 20 years later seems ridiculously low), so a deckhouse and any elaborate fittings on deck or below were counted out. With the draft restricted to some 40 percent of the beam there was

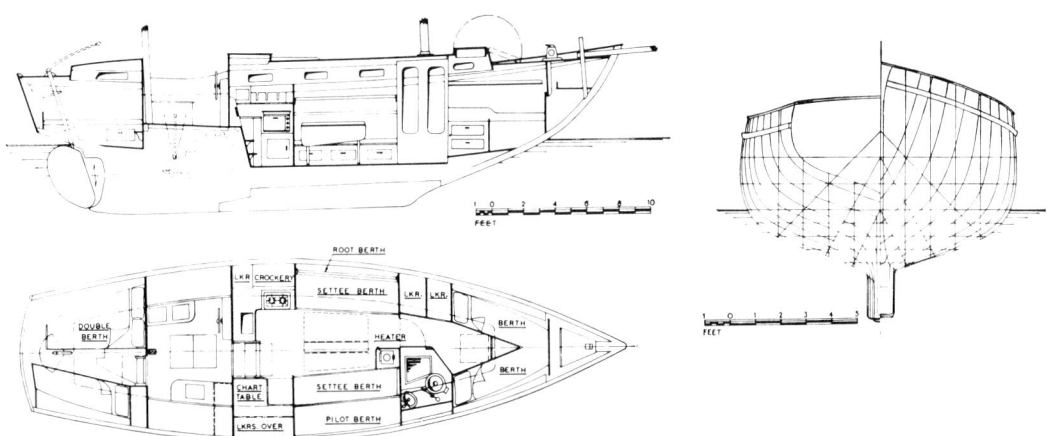

a need to make the vertical sides of the keel below the garboards as deep as permissable to reduce leeway when close-hauled. The garboard planks were accordingly made to butt against the keel sides without reverse curves. Also, as in all yachts with restricted draft, the ship must be stiff and never heel far in fresh winds, and her hull was therefore given a bold midsection with a firm turn to the bilges, almost in the manner of an East Coast fishing smack. This form of midsection has proved itself on many occasions when yachts built to this design have had to ride out severe weather off shore.

Good Hope was given a traditional long keel with moderate bow overhang (and a 10-inch wide plank type bowsprit), what I think is a pleasing sheer, and a bold stern with raised quarterdeck to accommodate the three berth after cabin. The characteristic carved mahogany rail around the quarterdeck was one of John's own ideas and the result of his own handiwork.

Many of the problems to be overcome in fitting in the accommodation in smaller yachts are much easier in a roomy hull of this size and depth. With a 7-inch footrail from the stem to the break at the quarterdeck, and 24-inch wide side decks, there was no problem below to obtain full sitting headroom over the saloon settees. A moderate height of coachroof from forward of the mainmast to the cockpit gave 6 feet 7 inches headroom throughout. In the after sleeping cabin where the hull runs up to the stern, limited depth was a problem, but the raised quarterdeck and a well cambered coachroof permitted headroom of 5 feet 6 inches.

The rest of the layout below is fairly conventional and can be seen in the accompanying plan. With a two-berth cabin forward, two settee berths plus a pilot berth in the saloon, and a double berth and single in the after cabin there are eight permanent berths for family and friends on short trips. I forget where the Labradors settled down, but the 6-foot 1-inch long self-draining cockpit with wide seats each side had an awning when needed, and could on occasion double up as a summer cabin.

Good Hope was very strongly built at Woodbridge on the River Deben by Whisstocks and launched in 1968. She proved a very docile boat to handle with little helm, and with a reasonable turn of speed considering her modest sail area. She drew much local admiration with the result that in 1970 Whisstocks received orders to build a sister ship, *Afrin*, for Dr Edward Bower (who bases her at Waldringfield), and another, *Matapan*, for Mr Cecil Barclay to be based on the Orwell. The following year, at Christchurch, Hampshire, Purbrook-Rossiters built another of these ketches which was lengthened some 30 inches aft to give more space to the stern cabin. With varnished topsides, rail and deck structures, *Cinnamon Lady*, as she is named, is a pleasing sight afloat.

The general design of these ketches appeared to be such an all round happy one for family cruising as well as blue water voyages that I decided to produce a ferrocement version for backyard construction. In the early 1970s there was a growing demand for ferro designs of around this size mainly from the energetic home builders Down Under and in South Africa, and the *Barrier Reef* ferro version of the *Good Hope* was the outcome.

The principal modifications to the wooden hull included reverse curves in the sections between the garboards and the keel to allow the pipe frames to be bent round them. The trough keel was also given greater depth so as to encapsulate the necessary bulk of cemented-in iron scrap and punchings to allow for the greater displacement of this hull. The construction specified a framework of ¾ inch diameter galvanised iron pipes spaced every 2 feet from stem to stern, looped around the stem, keel and decks to the edge of the coamings. Quarter inch solid rodding (standard concrete strengthening bars) was spaced every 3 inches both fore and aft and athwartships, wired together and covered with three layers both inside and out of ½-inch strong galvanised wire mesh. Whilst the decks, like the hull, were also of ferro with six layers of mesh, the main and after coachroofs, hatches and other deck structures were built traditionally of timber.

The accompanying outline diagram shows the general arrangement of this very strong construction, which is in fact a steel basket rendered water-tight by the infilling from inside and out of the mortar mix, aiming at a thickness in the topsides and bottom not in excess of 1⅛ inches. The

GOOD HOPE

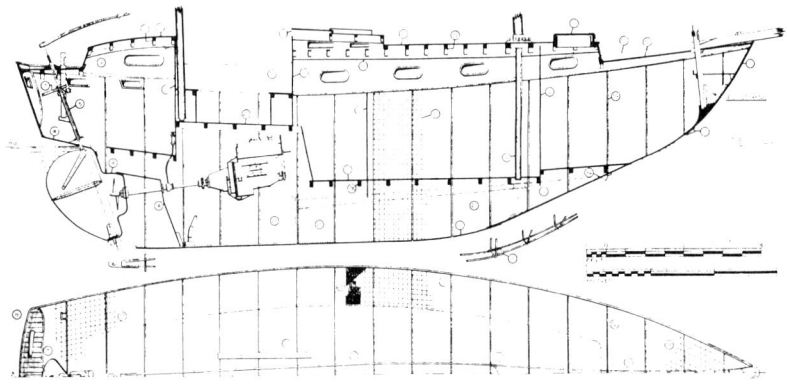

overall weight of this ferro version — which could vary with different builders' skill and interpretation of the specifications — ready to sail was calculated at 12.72 tonnes and a draft of 5 feet 6 inches. This may be compared with the *Good Hope*'s sailing displacement of 10.67 tonnes and draft, with shallower keel of under 4 feet 6 inches.

One of the Australian-built *Barrier Reef* class ketches, constructed by her owner in Queensland and named *Berenice*, became the family's only home for several years. The builder was an American who planned to set off for his home with his wife and family of three young children on a protracted voyage around the northern coasts of Australia, through the Torres Strait and the Timor Sea into the Indian Ocean and across the Atlantic by way of the Cape, taking three years or so.

Soon after they started the second-hand diesel which they had installed broke down and was never made to run again. Instead, the owner and his wife experimented with sails, sheets and tiller leads until they found that *Berenice* could be made to keep herself on course during most of the voyage, and they used no other steering devices. Crossing the Indian Ocean they encountered storm conditions and heavy seas in the north east monsoon weather. 'We left her hove-to (wrote the skipper some time later) and once lying a-hull (bare poles) during severe gales in the Indian Ocean, and later in the notorious Mocambique Channel, between Madagascar and the east coast of Africa. She took great care of us, while my wife never failed to produce hot meals each day on a non-gimballed stove.'

At Cape Town the yacht lay for some months while a fourth member of the crew (a boy) was born and the skipper worked on shore to pay for the rest of the voyage. In due course they crossed to America and reached the skipper's own home town, well contented with the long voyage and with the behaviour of their little ship.

GOLDEN HIND

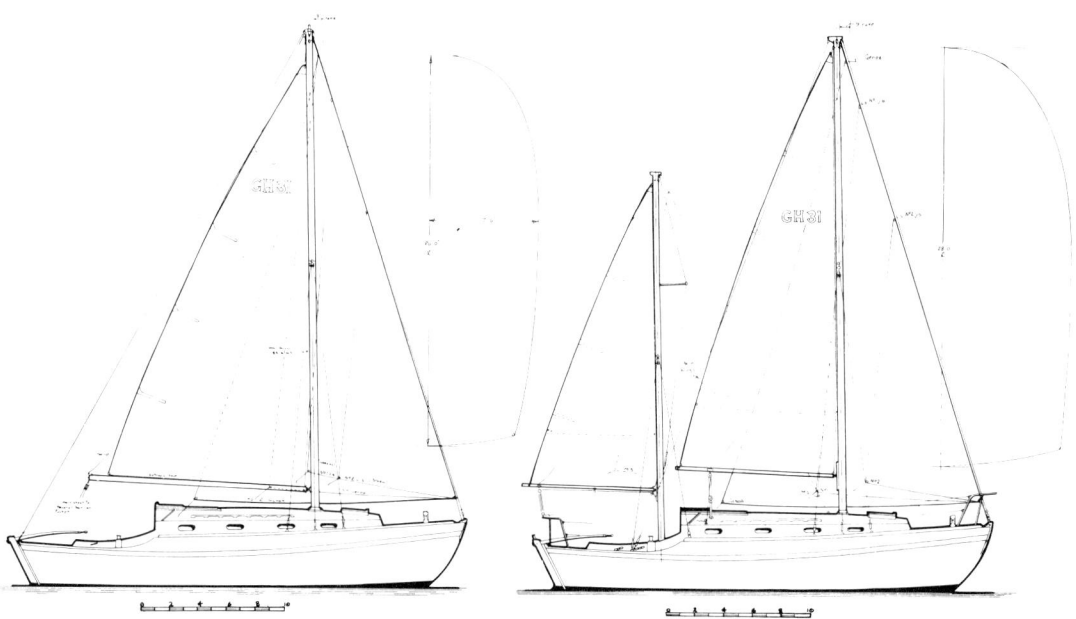

LOA	31.5ft
LWL	26.8ft
BEAM	9.0ft
DRAFT	3.8ft
DISPLACEMENT	12,600lbs
IRON KEEL	4,100lbs
BILGE KEELS(2)	580lbs
WKG SAIL AREA	370 sq ft
WITH GENOA	672 sq ft

THE GOLDEN HIND was designed exclusively for a Plymouth firm to produce as a standard line of comfortable, shoal draft bilge keelers with an eye to the family market. The first of these yachts was launched in 1965, and the original batches were 28.5 feet overall and 8.5 foot beam with single chines, and of marine-ply construction with the hull sheathed in resinglass. They made an appeal to those who looked for a comfortable, easy-to-manage cruising boat which could go anywhere and could squat on any level beach as if rooted to the spot, and after appearing at the Boat Show in London, they began to sell in numbers.

Very soon the demand rose for something a little bigger, with even more space below and headroom so as to make the yacht a family home. The design was accordingly redrawn to measure 31.5 feet on deck, 9.0 feet beam, with 6 feet 3 inches headroom in the saloon and 5 feet 9 inches in the forecabin, and was amended to have double chines each side, giving the hull a sweet run from bow to stern. In this form the *Golden Hind* 31, as it became known, was launched on a favourable tide which carried it eventually to a total number of 222 boats produced to the same design.

Early on, with the death of the original firm's principal, the business was taken over by the yard manager, Terry Erskine, who moved to modern and larger premises in Plymouth, and continued to build *Golden Hinds* under the banner Terry Erskine Yachts. The boats had been designed and built with substantial scantlings so that they were traditionally strong throughout, and in more than one case were to prove themselves able to take a pounding on a coral reef or on a hard shore without being wrecked.

GOLDEN HIND

The ½ inch steel bilge keel plates saved more than one from having holes punched in the bottom, while underway these bilge keels were to prove how effective they could be in holding the boat up to windward, and furthermore, in damping down rolling before following seas.

Amongst those who chose a *Golden Hind* for their next boat it is significant to find a high proportion were from America and Canada, quite a few of them with grown up families who were attracted to these yachts as their retirement home with the world as their playground. A number of customers from across the Atlantic arrived at the Terry Erskine yard in Plymouth, where their new boat had been completed internally to their individual requirements, and after the launch and acceptance trials had

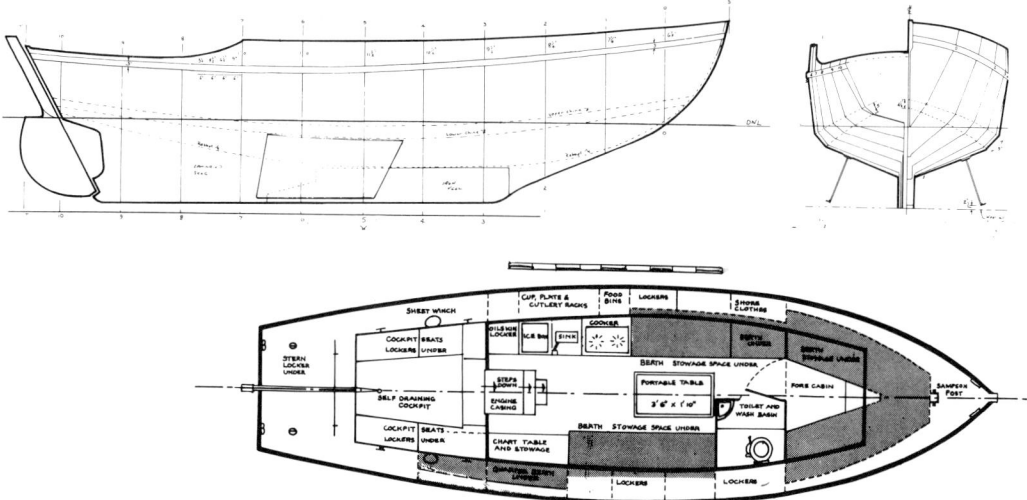

sailed away to 'do Europe' or spend a year or two in the Baltic or the Mediterranean before sailing across the Atlantic to their home waters.

This probably accounts in part for the number of Atlantic crossings made by *Golden Hind*s — to date recorded as 48 — a number of them being double crossings by European-based owners, and creating a record for any one class of production yacht. Doubtless because of their very sturdy construction and the care taken by the builders to meet every owner's personal requirements in the layout below decks, plus their well-proven seakeeping qualities, these yachts attracted a large number of the more adventurous types. Apart from middle-aged couples bent on retiring afloat, many were young couples cutting their ties on land and venturing forth on a year or two's wanderings before resettling; while others took their young children (and school books) along with them and introduced the youngsters to a sea life and an exciting variety of ports throughout the world.

That a *Golden Hind* could face severe weather at sea and take care of herself and her crew was shown time and again in letters that the builders received from their customers. For example, Mr Mark Ward and his wife with their two small daughters were on passage from Plymouth to Spain and Portugal in *Sea Fever* (GH No 120) and encountered two severe gales logged as Force 10. He wrote: 'The vessel has now become part of the family, she has proved herself in the two storms she encountered; she rode beautifully and suffered no damage from the sea. She is a fine boat, something to be proud of. In some of the heavy weather I saw other vessels nosing right down into the sea, large fishing boats making hardly any speed, and taking deep seas over the bows. *Sea Fever* did not; she took those waters in her stride and rode the waves with ease. She is a boat of which you and the designer can be justly proud.'

One couple from Canada who said they had never sailed before took delivery of their *Golden Hind* (No 104) and after being given lessons in sailing by the builders and the Plymouth Sailing Club, set off on a 10,000-mile cruise. This took them to Spain, Gibraltar, North African ports and the Canary Islands, followed by a 29-day crossing of the Atlantic to Barbados, whence they proceeded up the East Coast of America to their home ground at Port Stanley, Ontario. Here they sold their *Golden Hind* for a later version in which, nothing daunted (they felt they knew how to sail now) they set their course back to England via the Azores, only to retrace their previous voyage across the Atlantic a third time, and set off for an extended world cruise. Surely a fine example of wanderlust fraught with sea fever!

From the many letters received by the builders were accounts of others going on through the Panama Canal to explore the South Seas; how some settled with their families to their dream of a 'new life' in New Zealand or on one of the islands, while others — the number is not recorded — continued on a leisurely cruise of several years to encompass the world and all it has to offer. The Terry Erskine correspondence files over the years held a wealth of personal stories of nostalgic plans and adventures.

To meet a rising demand the builders turned over part of their works to producing *Golden Hinds* in moulded resinglass (GRP) as an alternative to the marineply version. These hulls were hand laid-up in a separate building under regulated temperature conditions to Lloyds standards, and were an immediate success. As with the wooden boats their scantlings were all on the substantial side, with hardwood stringers, chines and floor frames glassed in with the hull. Decks, coachroof, deck beams and all interior joinerwork were finely finished in hardwoods, so that there was little indication below decks of a GRP hull.

The *Golden Hind* series undoubtedly filled a need amongst the cruising fraternity who were not attracted to racing, but looked for an all-round comfortable and roomy boat that could lie at half-tide moorings and in dry harbours, yet could face all the hard weather likely to be met in all the Seven Seas. These boats have been aptly described as sailing caravans, while one writer described them as the Morris Minor of the yachting world:

both descriptions, I think, highly appropriate for this general-purpose boat.

In a changing yachting scene the *Golden Hind* 31 could not be expected to last for ever, and with the present day demand for ever larger and more comfortable yachts, and the increasing acceptance of steel for yacht construction, it was inevitable that the GH 31 should be superceded by a 39-foot version with an all-steel hull.

IDLE DUCK

LOA	34.0ft
LWL	31.25ft
BEAM	11.0ft
DRAFT	3.5ft with CB 6.33ft
DISPLACEMENT	20,800lbs
LEAD KEEL	5,240lbs
WKG SAIL AREA	595 sq ft
WITH GENOA	820 sq ft
THAMES M'MT	15 tons

BRIAN KELLEY, an experienced cruising man, and his wife kept their yacht in the half tide harbour of Tayport, in Fife. She was a lean 39-foot long sloop built at the German Baltic port of Travemünde in 1926, and in the half tide harbour the almost liquid mud enabled her to bury her deep keel and usually settle upright. For many years the Kelleys had been in the habit of making their summer cruise a crossing of the North Sea to their favourite haunts in the Baltic. Their yacht was undoubtedly fast, but like most of her slender type of craft, she liked to sail on her ear and was always very wet in a breeze, and sometimes the North Sea crossing could be anything but pleasant.

On a mooring close by in the same harbour lay a yacht which could be described as the very antithesis of the Kelleys': a broad beamed, transom sterned centreboarder with wide decks and knee-high bulwarks. She was called *Scoter* and was then owned by Colin Grierson, a marine artist who lived in Tayport. As the two dissimilar yachts often sailed in company down the Tay the Kelleys could not help admiring the way the centreboarder hardly heeled to a breeze and kept her decks dry, while their own yacht lay over and sliced through the seas with decks streaming, even

IDLE DUCK

though their aquatic pencil usually showed her long counter to the waddling duck.

There came a time when the Kelleys decided they had had enough of sailing in wet pants at an uncomfortable angle, and would have a boat built for their retirement on something like the *Scoter*'s lines. After long discussions and perusals of boating magazines and catalogues they decided to ask me to design it for them.

In an early part of this book I described how I had coveted *Scoter* when she lay at her moorings outside Ipswich docks back in the 1920s, and how she had influenced me years later when I came to design my first *Lone Gull* in 1938. *Scoter* had been built as long ago as 1894 by Howard at Maldon, and it is said she originally carried a bawley's rig of boomless mainsail with a long gaff, a big working topsail above, and a very long bowsprit. She measured 32.5 feet from stem to transom with 11.0-foot beam and 3 foot draft, and had no ballast on her outside wood keel and only a few slabs of lead stowed inside. To counteract this her cabin was divided down the centre by a huge case housing a 10-foot rectangular centreplate of ¾ inch iron. To handle the weight of this there was a wheel in the cockpit with curved spokes, like a Dutchman's windlass, and it was hard work winding up the heavy plate.

Colin Grierson had died, but through the kindness of Mrs Grierson who still ran the yacht with the family, I was able to refer to *Scoter*'s lines, which Colin had taken off her. Because in a tidal harbour every extra inch of draft curtailed sailing time on the tide, the Kelleys asked that the draft of their new boat should not exceed 3 feet 6 inches. I was adamant that she must have sufficient weight on an outside keel to make her stable and self-recoverable from a knockdown.

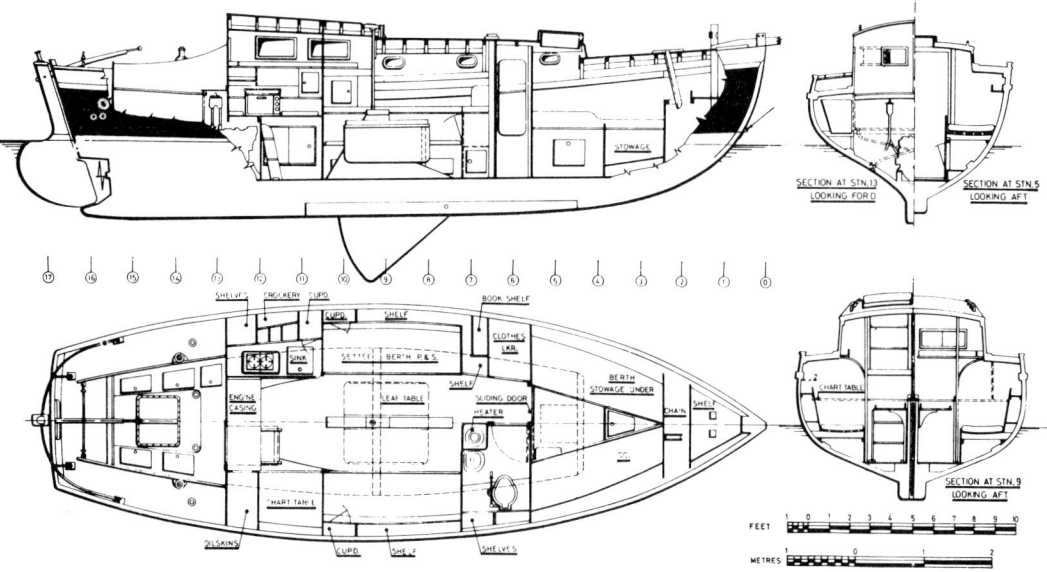

IDLE DUCK

This commission gave me great pleasure, as I had a chance to devise an updated version of the old boat I had coveted so much (before I had even learnt to sail) and benefitted from the knowledge we had gained about centreboard yachts since *Scoter* had been launched. In all other respects *Idle Duck*'s hull followed closely the lines of *Scoter* but we added 18 inches in length to make her 34 feet on deck, but with the same beam. It was found impossible within the limit of draft to mould the necessary weight of ballast in an iron keel, and a lead keel of some 2.38 tonnes was accordingly agreed upon.

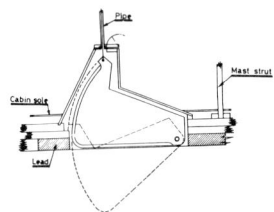

There was no need therefore to fit a heavy iron centreplate as part of the yacht's ballast, and a neat wooden board was designed to work inside a case which supported the saloon leaf table. A lip on the afterside of the

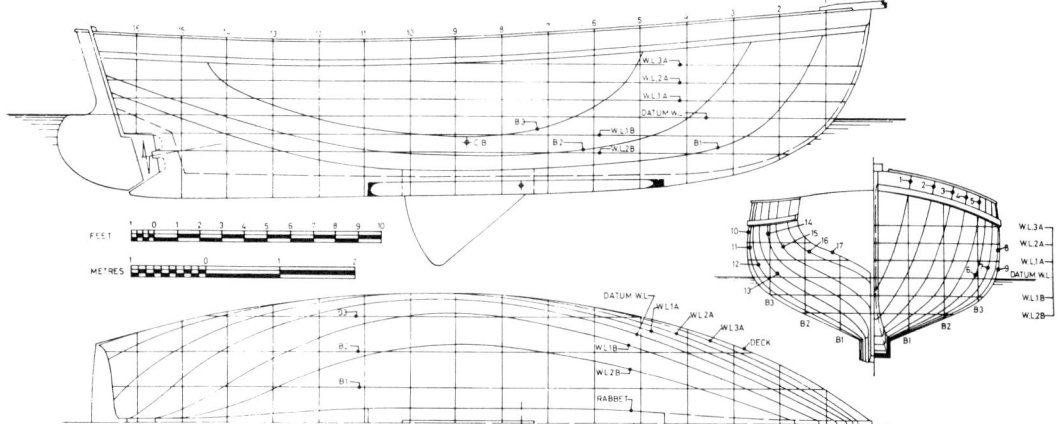

top part of the board was designed to come to rest on part of the wood keel when fully lowered, so as to stop the board from swinging right down should the hauling line come adrift. What can happen if a stop of this kind is not fitted (and many of the older centreboard yachts were culprits in this respect) was shown when a yacht with a heavy iron centreplate was thrashing up the Bristol Channel in a strong wind and the lifting cable of the plate suddenly let go. The plate dropped right down on its pivot bolt with a heavy thud, leaving only a small triangle of itself inside the keel slot. As the yacht drove to leeward with excessive leeway the plate buckled at the keel and appeared just under the surface to windward like a rusty looking stingray! The yacht had to be put on the yard slip once she got in, and the badly buckled plate taken out and straightened again: an expensive lesson.

Idle Duck's wooden board was built up with three layers of well seasoned pitchpine in ⅝ inch fore and aft planks outside and ¾ inch vertical planks inside. A 60-pound slab of lead was inserted in the inner skin to take the board down. The planks were fastened throughout with Gripfast bronze nails driven flush, and the underside and chamfered-off after edge of the board was protected by a ¾ inch half round brass beading. Brian Kelley is skilful with tools and not only made a fine job of this built-up board himself, but also made the beautiful hollow mast in spruce.

Idle Duck was heavily built by James N Miller & Sons at St Monance, Fife in 1970, with 1⅜ inch iroko planking, copper fastened to English oak timbers 2 inches by 1½ inches closely spaced at 7 inches throughout, with 2½ inch by ⅝ inch bronze floor-frames at every third timber. An oak hog 4 inches moulded depth and sided 24 inches was bolted to the top of the 5-inch moulded oak keel 15 inches wide amidships, allowing a 4-inch width of landing each side for fastening the garboard strakes. Decks of marine ply were covered with teak planking to the curve of the covering boards, a traditional touch rarely seen these days. Below decks the accommodation is conventional for four persons with the fine teak finish associated with the St Monance yard. With 6 feet 10 inches headroom under the main hatch and 6 feet 1 inch under the deck beams there is a noticeable air of light and space.

Writing of his new ship Brian Kelley said: '*Idle Duck* has turned out what we wanted. We find 'Duckers' dry and kindly at sea whether to windward or running before a North Sea swell. Although we were prepared to accept a rather slow ship, we find that she is much faster both in smooth water and in the rough stuff than we dared hope for. On a wind when it is steady in strength she will sail herself as long as the wind lasts; on any other point of sailing she gives time to light the Primus, plot a position etc. We haven't yet had to face a full gale, but from her behaviour in rough conditions and from experiments in heaving-to in winds of Force 6 and 7, we are confident that when heaving-to is really necessary, she will be dry and safe.'

KYLIX

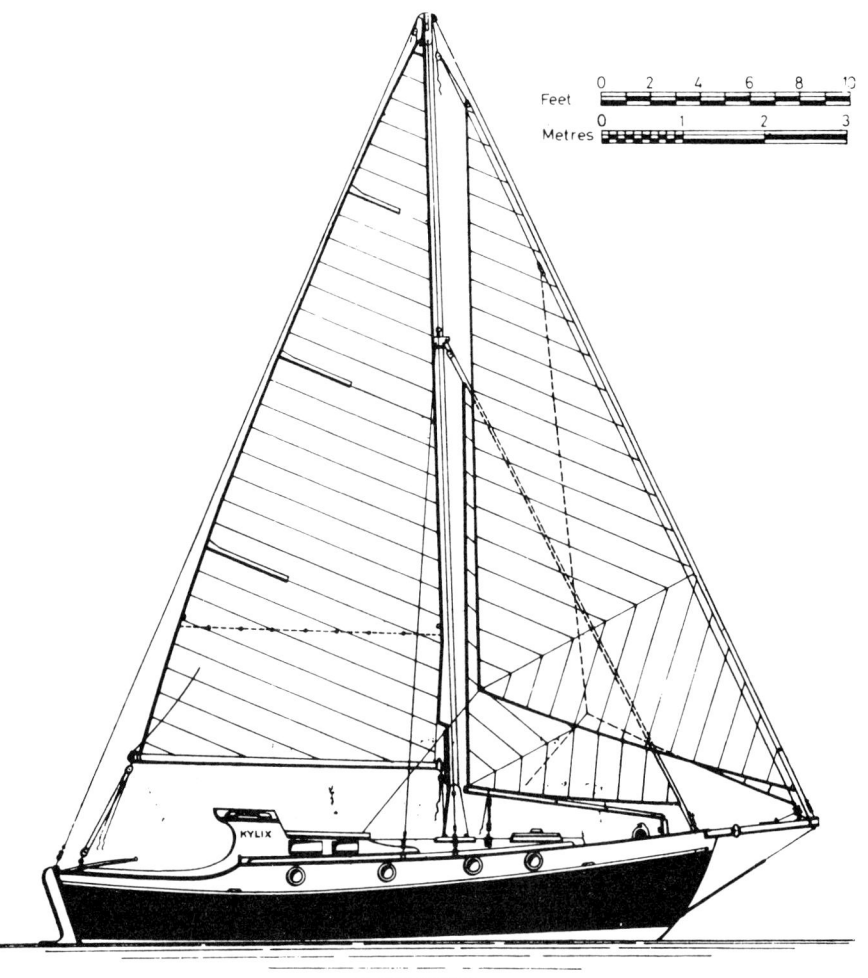

LOA	27.0ft
LWL	23.50ft
BEAM	8.20ft
DRAFT	3.0ft
	plate down 6.25ft
DISPLACEMENT	9,500lbs
IRON KEEL	2,700lbs
WKG SAIL AREA	306 sq ft
THAMES M'MT	7 ton

AFTER RETIREMENT, and one or two house moves, my wife and I settled in that charming little Suffolk town of Woodbridge. With the prettily wooded Deben river and the old quay only a short distance from our house the old itch to get afloat made itself felt again. Since *Lone Gull II* was sold we had been without a boat for the past eight years, and this seemed an ideal opportunity to build something for my retirement years.

The river almost dries out near the town quay, and lower down where a yacht could remain afloat moorings were like gold dust, but a site a mile down off Kyson hard was offered me provided I laid the mooring myself. This was at the entrance to Loder's Cut, a straight channel which had been dug through the saltings before the railway came to Woodbridge to enable the timber schooners, coal brigs and barges to escape the shoals of Troublesome Reach (treacherous for yachts even today) on their way

KYLIX

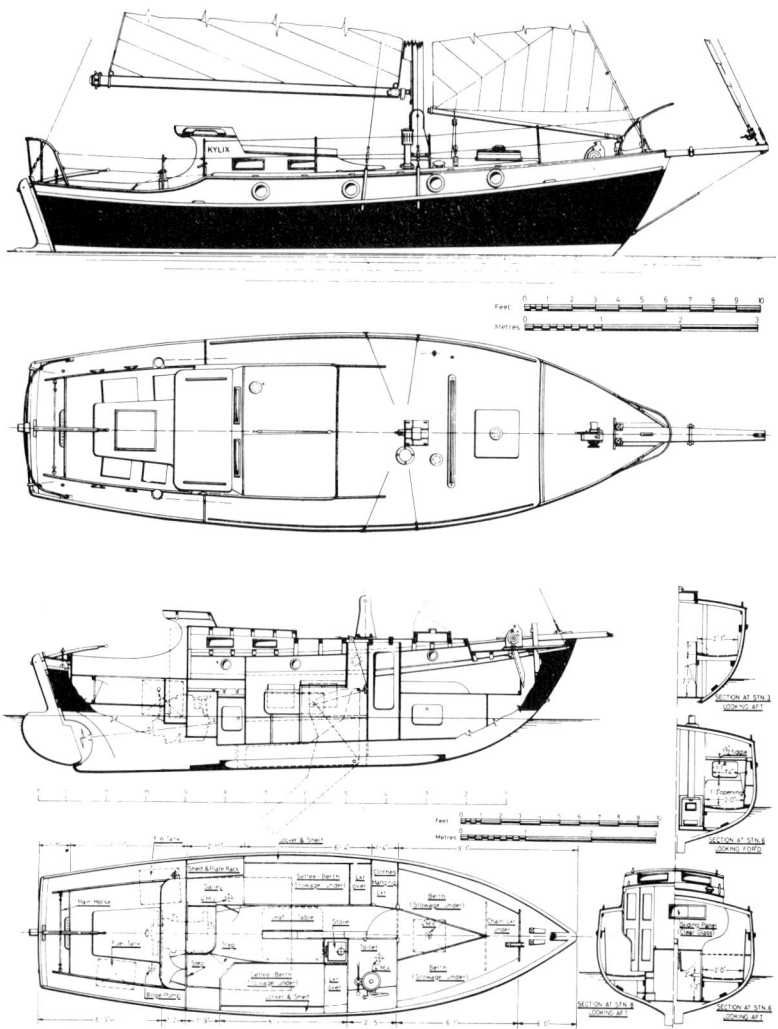

up to the town quay.

Soundings showed that there was no more than 3 feet at low water around the mooring, while at the Deben entrance the same depth was found in the channel between the shingle banks at LW springs. Bearing in mind these conditions and the inevitable failing in the strength of a 70-year-old, I planned Kylix as a lightweight centreboarder with not more than 3 feet hull draft, and with light gear for ease of handling.

Her design was a development of my 25-foot *Cockler* class centreboarders, with an easy bow entrance and a fine run up aft to a transom well clear of the water. The L-shape centreplate of ½ inch steel worked, like the *Cockler*'s, in a case supporting the cabin table with the hauling wire led up inside the case extension (which supported the mast tabernacle) to a 3 to 1 purchase led to the cockpit. The top of the case could be opened

up to inspect the stainless steel wire and to clear the plate if jammed with mud and stones. A gallon of old sump oil poured into the case about once a season kept the plate working smoothly and disgusted any marine borers which tried their luck.

With a plank type bowsprit 4 feet outboard — on which the double chain roller fitting carried the CQR anchor clear of the stem — the Wykeham Martin furling jib was set, with the forestays'l working on a boom. The main boom had normal worm roller reefing gear. This was before the advent of slab reefing for the main and reefing roller jib gears, otherwise I think I should have fitted them to this boat for greater ease in sail handling.

Kylix (Greek for a shallow drinking vessel) took just a year abuilding at Fred Smeeth's boatyard on the upper Stour at Dedham, and was launched off Woodbridge Quay in 1971. Her planking, stem, sternpost and deadwoods were of iroko which had been seasoning in the yard for the previous ten years, and she was built with a moderate displacement to stand grounding on hard sands. She had the raised flush midship deck with a break just forward of the double-coaming forehatch like *Lone Gull II*'s, and the raised main hatch carried on after extension which we called the loco-cab and formed a welcome wind and spray hood over the fore end of the cockpit.

The entrance to the cabin was to starboard of the 15bhp Lister diesel together with the open oilskin locker, while the galley was opposite to port. The four-berth layout was conventional, as seen in the plan, with a slow-burning caravan type stove to starboard of the centreboard case — a very welcome feature on cold days. *Kylix* was a delightful little boat to sail and never overtaxed me when singlehanded; she never pulled hard on the helm and would sail under almost any combination of sails.

The design appeared to appeal to a number of yachtsmen familiar with this type of boat, with the result that one firm, Bure Marine at their Cobholm yard, Great Yarmouth, received orders to build nine others of this design (but all a little different) for owners in the UK and on the Continent. Unhappily for the trade, good seasoned timber was becoming harder to find; fine logs were no longer imported as deck cargo but inside containers which limited their length below what was needed by a yard for, say, a 28-foot yacht. Prices of timber were rocketing, while shipwright craftsmen were leaving the boatyards for better paid jobs elsewhere. Except where expense was no object, the day of the custom-built wooden yacht was drawing to a close.

Kylix might have been expected to see me out, but when on the foredeck stowing the stays'l in a sudden hail squall one day, fortunately while in the river, I slipped under the windlass and broke a leg at the ankle and under the kneecap. It took a long time to heal and left me very clumsy in getting on or off any boat. My singlehanded sailing days were finished, and I felt too much of a liability to sail aboard friends' boats. After all, I had had over half a century of boat owning and sailing and surely ought to be satisfied.

A move to a house overlooking the entrance to the Blackwater at West Mersea where many craft — fishermen, yachts, dinghies, barges, coasters, harbour tugs and the local inshore lifeboat — can be seen underway winter and summer, has been a welcome relaxation. If at times it is a temptation just to sit with the binoculars and watch, the window of my study, where most of the work is done, has, fortunately, no river view!

NOONTIDE

LOA	32.0 ft
LWL	26.1 ft
BEAM	9.5 ft
DRAFT	3.9 ft
DISPLACEMENT	14,120 lbs
BALLAST	3,900 lbs
WKG SAIL AREA	463 sq ft
WITH GENOA	661 sq ft
THAMES M'MT	10 tons

BECAUSE IN Holland there has been a scarcity of good home grown timber suitable for building ships and small craft, the Dutch have been constructing their barges and ferryboats and yachts in steel from the turn of the century. Acceptance of steel for yacht building has been slow to mature in the United Kingdom, as good boat building timbers have until recently been plentiful and British yacht yards have been able to satisfy their customers who 'like wood for its own sake' with well seasoned timber and first class workmanship.

In the past generation, however, yachtsmen have had to become inured to the acceptance of resinglass hulls and the increasing difficulties of having wooden yachts built, and have begun to accept the evident advantages of a steel yacht: the inherent strength in the hull, freedom from leaks from the decks and below, and the comparative ease with which damage to a steel hull can be repaired. With the introduction of epoxy resins and other rust inhibitors which can be applied to the hull while it is being built, the old bogey of rust and corrosion in a steel boat has lost much of its menace. Some Dutch yacht building yards are understood to offer a six-year guarantee against corrosion on a newly built hull.

For the home builder who has learnt welding skills and has the equipment, construction of a steel hull calls for far less labour and fewer shipwright skills than a conventional wooden boat, while the cost of the materials to build the hull is appreciably less. As these ideas spread, there arose at least the beginnings of a demand for a simple design of cruising yacht for steel construction with accommodation for four or five which any capable welder could build in his back garden.

Way back in 1961, I recalled, we had produced plans for the 30-foot *Waterwitch* for the *Yachting Monthly* home builder series. She was a single chine ketch (or sloop) for construction in marine-ply, with bilge keel plates and a 3 foot draft. The hull was something on the lines of a barge, but with a V'd bottom and a central iron ballast keel to bring her back on her feet in the event of a knockdown. I believe something approaching one hundred of these *Waterwitch* class boats have been built, mostly by

NOONTIDE

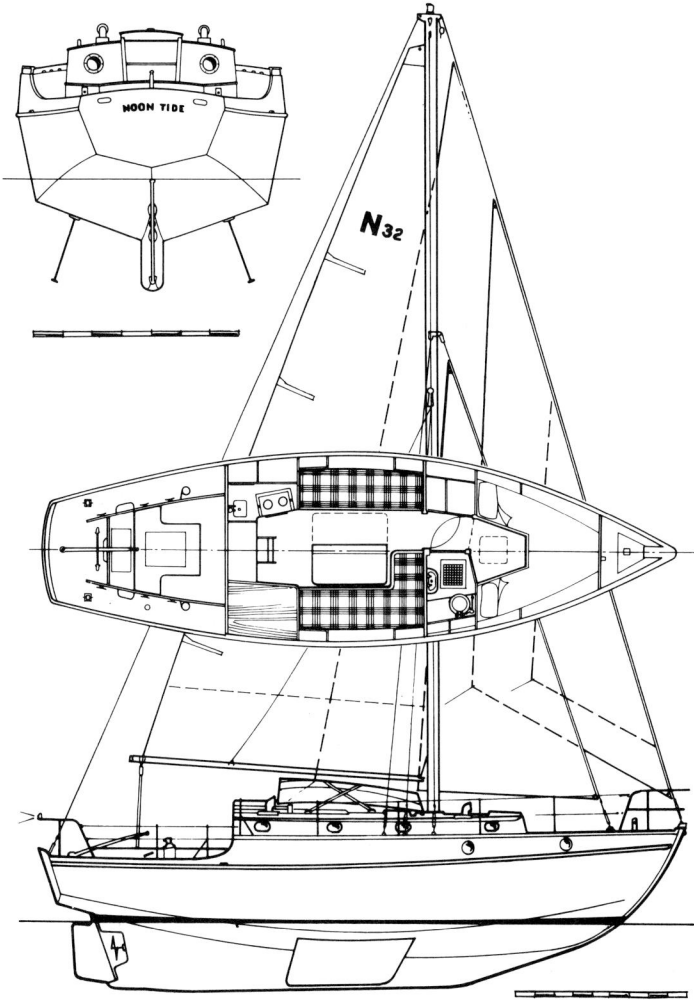

their owners, since the Eventide Owners Association took over distributing the plans, and they have been seen in many parts of the world, while at least two have made a circumnavigation.

After discussions with builders and other designers my ideas crystallised in the form of an updated version of the *Yachting Monthly* designs, but lengthened a little for the rudder to be mounted inboard of the transom, and with a foot more beam and increased depth of hull; in short, a bigger, roomier and a more powerful boat. The *Noontide* 32 was the outcome.

With a full length keel and more draft than on the *Waterwitch*, the family resemblance to the *Golden Hind* 31 was unmistakeable, and like the latter class the bilge keel plates were not essential to the design. The *Noontide* would work her way to windward without them, but they would be optional for owners who required them for shoal waters and local conditions. There is little woodwork in the construction of the *Noontide* hull: the topsides and bottom plating are of 4mm steel, upper strakes (from rubrail to deck edge) are 3mm, and decks, cabin top and coamings, cockpit sides, sole and bridge deck are likewise of 3mm plating. The chine bars and three longitudinal stringers each side are 32mm by 6mm flat bars, while transverse frames are flat bars welded edge on to the hull plating 44mm by 6mm at 310mm (24in) spacing.

The trough keel has 5mm sides and a 10mm baseplate and contains iron scrap ballast cemented in with bitumastic top levelled off to drain down into the bilge sump with strum box at lowest part. The bilge keels, approximately 6 feet by 2 feet 3 inches, are 12mm plate welded to a 120mm by 12mm top flange with a bottom flange 63mm by 12mm, to prevent digging into mud or soft sand. Tanks for fresh water and diesel fuel hold some 65 gallons (295 litres) each. The general construction has been devised to make welding and assembly as convenient as practicable for the amateur builder. The hull is very strong and could be said to be tough enough to stand up to more hammering on a coral reef or a rocky shore than a wooden one of the same size.

The layout below decks is conventional and well tried, with a two-berth cabin forward; a heads large enough for sea toilet (or chemical), washbasin and shower; with a double clothes hanging locker to port. In the saloon the two settee berths have lockers and shelves at the back of them, while the starboard L-shaped settee with leaf table can be arranged to convert to a double berth if desired. Alternatively, the forward part could be omitted if preferred to make room for a small cabin heater: paraffin, charcoal, gas or coal. Also, the chart table aft could be arranged to lift up to allow for a quarter berth. The cockpit is self-draining with a seat-bridge deck over the diesel engine and large flush hatch in the sole for access. Ventilation below decks is taken care of by four Dorade type (box-trap) ventilators and translucent clams where required. Headroom under the coachroof beams is not less than 6 feet.

The first of this class, **Water Ratty**, was built in 1982 by the builders of the Bay Class range of steel yachts, Conyer Marine Ltd, at their Conyer Quay yard near Sittingbourne, Kent. This yacht was given the high class finish both on the outside of the hull and topsides as well as in the joinerwork below decks on which the builders pride themselves. In trials she showed herself a well balanced, easily handled little ship with plenty of power to stand up to her sails in a breeze.

Water Ratty's bilge keel plate flanges were attached to the hull with small bolts in pairs, to enable them to be removed for trials. It was found that the keels in place seemed to make little difference to the yacht's speed, but when sailing on the wind they did help the yacht to hold up well. Their roll-damping effect before following seas could not be put to the test in the river, but with this form of V-bottom hull rolling badly down wind would probably never be as much of a problem as with a slack bilged, round bottomed yacht.

GULF STREAM

LOA	42.0ft
LWL	33.5ft
BEAM	12.0ft
DRAFT	4.5ft
BALLAST	9,700lbs
WKG SAIL AREA	810 sq ft
LIGHT WEATHER	1337 sq ft
THAMES M'MT	22 tons

FOR THOSE WHOSE pockets would run to a larger yacht with ample room below decks, the *Gulf Stream* 42 was planned with an eye to both long distance blue water cruising, and for exploring the shallow waters of estuaries, creeks, upper reaches of tidal rivers, and perhaps island lagoons. For beaching and visiting harbours that dry out, the twin bilge keel plates will ensure that the yacht will settle upright on the ground. These bilge keels are not, however, essential to the yacht's design; they may be omitted altogether if a slightly reduced performance to windward under sail is acceptable.

Considerably larger than the *Noontide* 32, the double-chined hull of this ketch is constructed almost entirely in steel, and for the technically minded the following details will give a rough guide to the method of construction. Her hull, from deck edge to the keel and the transom, is of 5mm plating, the keel sides being 6mm and baseplate 10mm. The sides of the keel are carried up some 30mm above the garboards plating to ensure ease of inside welding. The stem and stern bars are both of 65mm

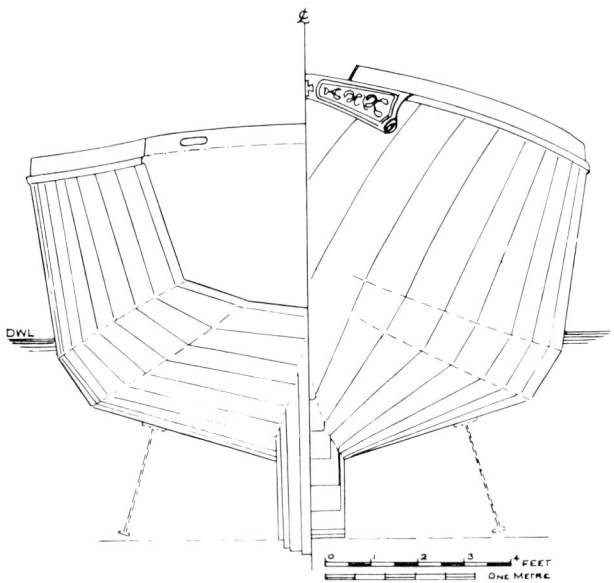

by 12mm flat bars, and flanged 5mm floorplates are stationed at each transverse angle frame 40mm by 40mm by 5mm, which is edge-welded to the hull plating at 610mm spacing. These frames are slotted to take four longitudinal stringers aside running from stem to stern.

The maindeck is 4mm with coachroof and coamings of 3mm plate. The angle bar main deck beams are slotted to take angle bar longitudinals from bow to stern. The 6-foot 3-inch long self-draining cockpit is built up as a steel box with 3mm sole, sides and bench tops, the sole supported on angle bearers. Drains of a generous diameter are crossed over from the forward corners of the cockpit sole. The ballast, consisting of 9700 pounds of iron scrap is cemented within the keel trough, the top being levelled off on a slope aft and bitumen covered to the pump well. In compartments aft of the ballast the keel has space either for additional fresh water storage of some 150 gallons or for use as a sludge storage tank.

The layout on deck and below has been planned for five adults to cruise extensively, or for seven for shorter periods. The deck saloon above the engine-room has the settee with leaf table (which is convertible to a double berth) and storage lockers to starboard, with the galley, fridge and oilskins locker to port. Down three steps is a passageway with a full size chart table to port (amidships where less motion is felt at sea) and opposite the roomy heads with toilet, shower and a second oilskin hanging locker. Forward is the owner's double berth stateroom with a passage berth to port leading into the two-berth forecabin. A watertight bulkhead with access hatch separates this from the cable locker and forepeak stowage.

On deck the wide bowsprit carries the double chain roller well clear of

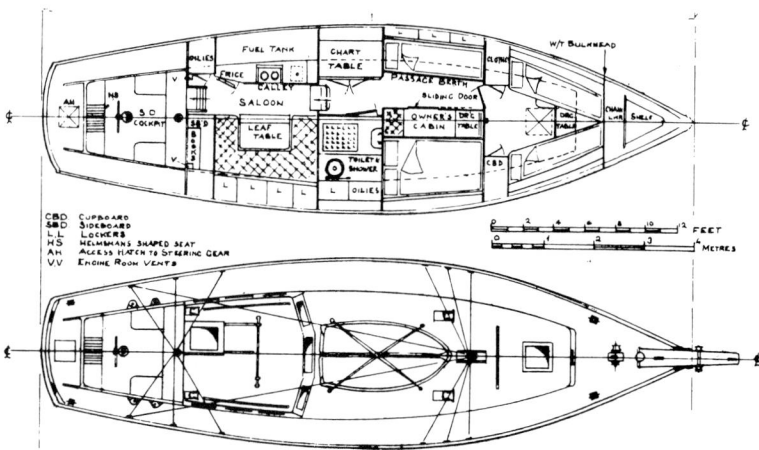

the stem, with a substantial 12-inch high steel samson post at its heel, adequate for most warps when lying abreast on piles or entering a lock. Roller reefing gear on the jib with the forestays'l working on a boom, and slab reefing on the mainsail with worm roller reefing for the mizzen is planned to make working this ketch as trouble-free as can be. The BMC Leyland 4-cylinder diesel (or similar) is installed beneath the forward end of the deck saloon, beneath a flush fitting hatch. Fuel and water tanks are to port and starboard, and the engine exhaust line is led up to a mixer-silencer under the bridge deck and thence by a swan neck to the transom outlet. Ventilation is taken care of by two cowl heads, one inhaling the other extracting from the engineroom, and box-trap ventilators for the galley and accommodation below in addition to limpet-type vents with translucent tops on deck where required.

At all locations where brass or gunmetal skin fittings are to be attached to the hull plating (seacocks, propeller shaft etc.) soft sacrificial zinc plates are to be fitted in close proximity, while any bronze outlet (galley, toilet etc.) is not fitted direct to the hull plating, but to an extension steel pipe leading inboard where it can be inspected for corrosion. With such proper precautions a steel hull need not waste itself away in inaccessible parts.

BAY CLASS YACHTS

EXCEPT FOR quantity production lines of yachts which are successfully moulded in resinglass, the advantages of steel construction for vessels over, say, 33 feet (10 metres) in length have already been mentioned in this book. Conyer Marine Ltd have been building steel yachts and small commercial vessels for many years at their Kentish yard, on a site where countless barges, tugs and small coasters have been launched into the creek since the early years of the 19th century.

The Spears family who own the yard have specialised in producing yachts with high quality smooth finish to their steel hulls together with an equally high class joinerwork both on deck and below. The firm's consultant naval architect, Lt Commander Robert Hundy, RNR (rtd), before joining the firm had spent 17 years after his war service working in Holland at a yard where sailing and power yachts, as well as varieties of commercial craft, were built, and he was naturally well versed in steel construction and the latest Dutch techniques.

Conyer Marine had introduced a line of cruising yachts known as the Bay Class, and when they invited me to offer designs for inclusion in this range in collaboration with Bob Hundy, I was glad to have the opportunity to learn more of the techniques of small craft steel construction

from my knowledgeable colleague, on the principle that an old dog is never too old to learn new tricks.

The Spears-Hundy-Griffiths consortium has resulted in some very pleasing cruising yachts being launched into Conyer creek for a variety of owners. Once the design of the hull has been approved each yacht is planned, both on deck and in the accommodation arrangements below, to meet her respective owner's requirements. In a range which has varied up to the present from 36 feet to 58 feet on deck the variety in the layout details of the galley, saloon, stateroom, forecabin, engine-room, position

BAY CLASS YACHTS

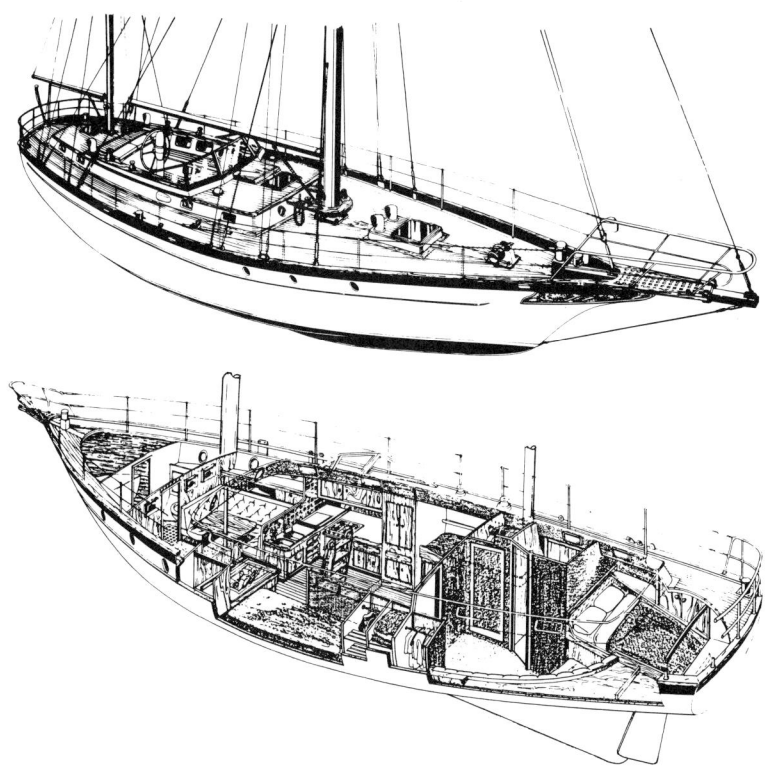

BAY CLASS YACHTS

of the cockpit and arrangements on deck to meet the owner's personal wishes has sometimes provided a challenge to both designers and builders. But the results have been successful as noted at various boat shows in the UK and on the Continent.

As examples of Conyer-Hundy-Griffiths productions perspective views of two yachts are reproduced here, the 39.4-foot *Tobago Bay* with cutter rig, and the 44-foot *Bay of Islands* ketch. *Tobago Bay*'s other measurements are 31.3 feet WL, 11.2 feet beam, 5.5 feet draft on 13.0 tonnes displacement with 3.5 tonnes ballast in the keel. Working sail area is 775 square feet and 1036 square feet with genoa. The accommodation of this boat is well planned with two-berth forecabin, toilet with shower the full width of the ship, saloon with two pilot berths in addition to dinette arrangement for six, deck saloon over the engine compartment, with galley and alternative inside steering position, and a spacious self-draining cockpit aft.

The larger *Bay of Islands* ketch with centre cockpit and double berth cabin aft measures 44.0 feet on deck, 34.6 feet WL, 12.5 feet beam and 5.8 feet (1.77m) draft on 16.25 tonnes displacement. The working sail area is 754 square feet and 1180 square feet with genoa. The cutout perspective view gives an idea of the extensive accommodation layout which the builders were able to work into this powerful yacht.

APPENDIX

TAKING OFF A BOAT'S LINES

WITH SO MANY of today's yachts coming off production moulds, the hull lines are rarely available to their proud owners. As explained elsewhere, the yacht's plans are in any case the brain child of the designer and, therefore, his or his firm's copyright, which means that even if the lines plan comes into possession of someone else it will be illegal for him to use the plan to build a full-size replica, or to pass on the plans to another party to do so, without first obtaining the designer's written permission. For this there would normally be a fee. There is, however, no reason why a yacht owner should not take off the lines of his boat, or some other craft to record the subject for posterity, or to make a half or full model for his own satisfaction. It is not difficult to take off the lines of a small yacht or fishing boat's hull given reasonably favourable conditions, and the methods described here have been used with success in recording the lines of numbers of yachts as well as fast disappearing types of local fishing and commercial craft.

The technique might appear to some purists as haphazard and a trifle crude where a vessel cannot be hauled out onto a level floor, but a practical approach with a straight eye and one, better two, willing helpers can produce accurate enough results with the simplest tools. These comprise the following:

1. Plumb bob and line
2. Three straight wooden battens from 5 feet to 8 feet in length and about 1½ inches by ½ inch
3. A 33-foot or 50-foot linen tape measure. (A steel tape is not favoured as it will tend to rust, and the figures are more difficult to read)
4. Blackboard chalks
5. Length of string for chalkline marker
6. Small spirit level
7. Adhesive tape to fix spirit level temporarily to battens
8. A two-foot (or builder's three-foot) folding rule
9. Loose leaf note pad, pencils, rubber

The ideal condition is for the vessel to be hauled out under cover in a dry shed, but life's not always like that, and in the case of a fishing boat or small commercial vessel you will more likely have to work on the foreshore or against a quay. As in all things, working becomes easier after a little practice, and it pays to start with quite a small boat such as a sailing dinghy which can be chocked up level and firm in a dry shed. For a larger boat an understanding helper will be needed to hold the tap measure, stretch the chalkline, and hold battens level and steady; while

APPENDIX

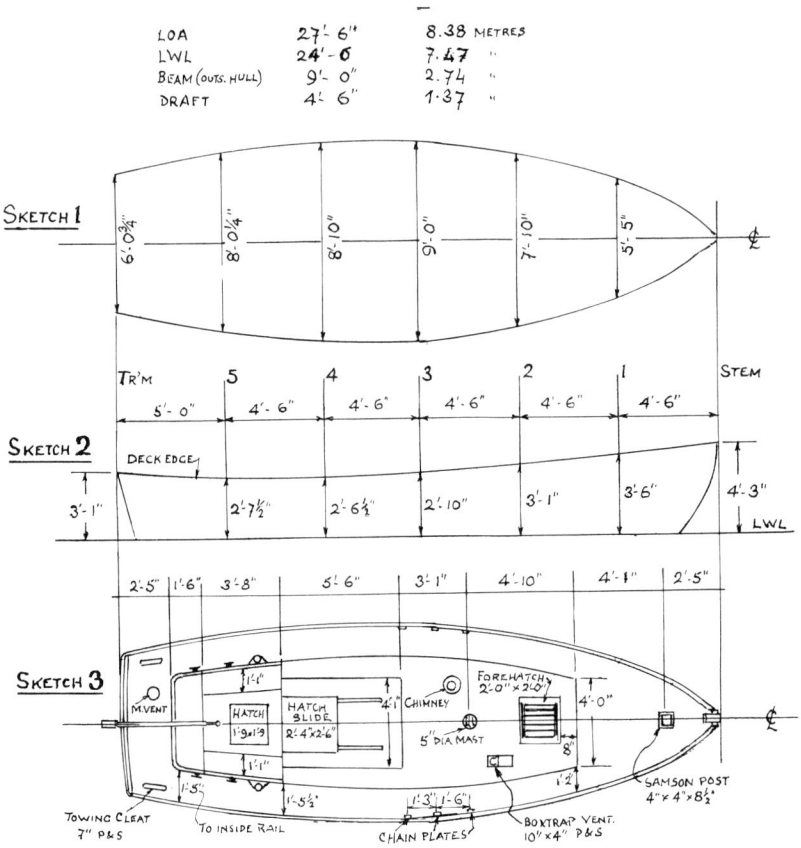

a second hand is also valuable for noting down all the measurements as they are called out.

As our working example we will take off the lines from a cruising sloop of traditional type, 27 feet 6 inches (8.38m) from stem to transom stern, which is to be legged up on the hard for our purpose. While the yacht is still afloat we divide the deck into six measured spaces by chalk lines drawn across the deck athwartships to the outside of the planking or deck edge, and note the measurements of these and across the transom stern. (Sketch 1)

The sheer height to the deck edge at each of these stations is next measured from a dinghy alongside by the folding rule held plumb with its lower end just touching the water (Sketch 2). This should be repeated on the other side as the boat might have a slight list (most boats have) and the mean of the measurements taken. The heights of the footrail or bulwarks at all the stations are noted, so that the resulting drawing will be the broadside view of the yacht's hull afloat on her actual load line (the LWL).

The yacht can now be put on the hard and her legs adjusted to the

APPENDIX

rigging so that she will settle as nearly upright as practicable, using the plumb bob on board. Until the tide leaves her we use the time noting the positions and measurements of deck fittings, hatches, coachroof, cockpit coamings, seats, ventilators, chain plates and so on, and from these data an accurate deck plan can be drawn (Sketch 3). If when the tide leaves her she has settled with her keel a few inches into the mud this can be dealt with without difficulty. The important thing is to work from one fixed datum line. This can be a chalk line stretched level from stem to stern and flicked to mark the hull at, say, midship deck level, or at the yacht's load waterline. For our purpose we will adopt this LWL.

If you are not good at making freehand sketches, not to worry; just make a rough sketch of any part to be recorded as nearly like the object as you can (eg rudder, tiller, cabin sides, hatches, samson post or bitts, stemhead fitting and so on) then insert on your sketch all its measurements. These can be used later to draw the items to scale on the plans. You cannot make a note of too many measurements.

With the yacht dried out, overboard we go in seaboots with rule, battens, plumb bob and notebook. The amount the yacht's keel has settled in the mud — perhaps two inches — is allowed for in the measuring, and its width obtained by tunnelling beneath and inserting the rule. Stem and sternpost rakes are checked with plumb bob and batten, and for the forefoot and bow profile the long batten is laid on the ground as an extension of the keel base, with a second batten held plumb with the fore side of the stemhead, and offsets are measured to the stem at any convenient regular spacing (Sketch 4). Measurements of the propeller gap and of the rudder and positions of pintles and gudgeon pins are similarly noted (Sketch 5), and with a note of the rabbet (rebate) line from bow to stern we can now make a correct broadside view (or elevation drawing) of the whole hull.

Next comes the job of taking off the curves of the hull from deck edge

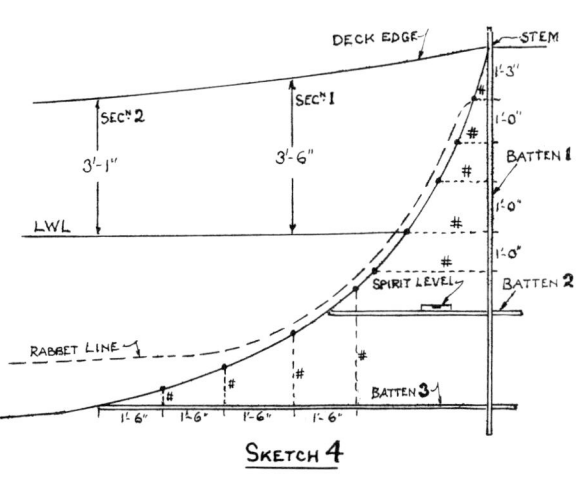

Sketch 4

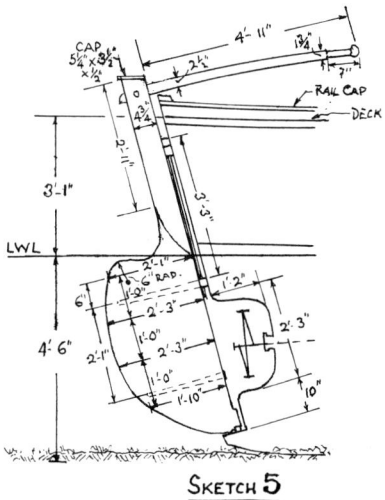

Sketch 5

APPENDIX

to keel at the marked stations, nos 1, 2, 3, 4, 5 and transom. If it has been shown that the bottom of the keel is 2 inches below the surface of the hard we can match this with the lower end of our upright batten. But if the submerged depth is uncertain, as in mud, we can take instead the rabbet line. While one helper holds the batten exactly plumb against the yacht's side at each station in turn, the measurer holds the shorter batten against the rabbet line exactly level (this is where the attached spirit level is needed) and marks off spots on both battens at regular, say 12-inch, intervals from the deck edge to the keel rabbet line.

Offset measurements are now taken from these marks to the hull in turn and noted (Sketch 6). For each level or waterline, which will be spaced at 12-inch intervals both above and below the LWL on the plan the respective measurements are also noted, so that the correct curve of each station (or section) will be obtained by connecting the points with a fair curve. On the half-breadth plan these level line points will be drawn in using a spline or sweep which will show the curves of the various waterlines as seen from above. As boats are all assumed to be identical on both sides (sometimes not strictly true, especially with wooden craft) only one side of the yacht's hull will therefore be shown. A method of measuring the transom is shown in Sketch 7. With a clinker-built or lapstrake boat, such as a Shetland sixern or a Yorkshire coble, the positions of the strakes are important on the drawing if the true character of the boat is to be recorded. The depths of the plank edges, or lands, beneath the deck edge or gunn'le must be noted and the appropriate positions spotted on the plan, thereby showing off the run of the strakes to advantage.

We now have sufficient data to enable us to make a scale drawing of the hull in elevation, a detailed deck plan with its fittings, and a body plan as viewed along the keel centreline with its five sections and transom stern. The plan can be drawn on squared paper, plain white, or tracing paper to any convenient scale, such as 1:24, 1:32 or 1:12 (Sketch 8). If

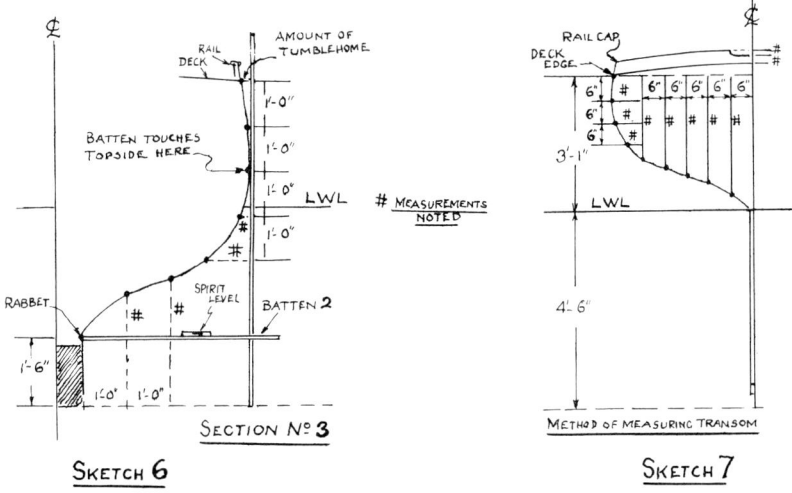

SKETCH 6

SKETCH 7

APPENDIX

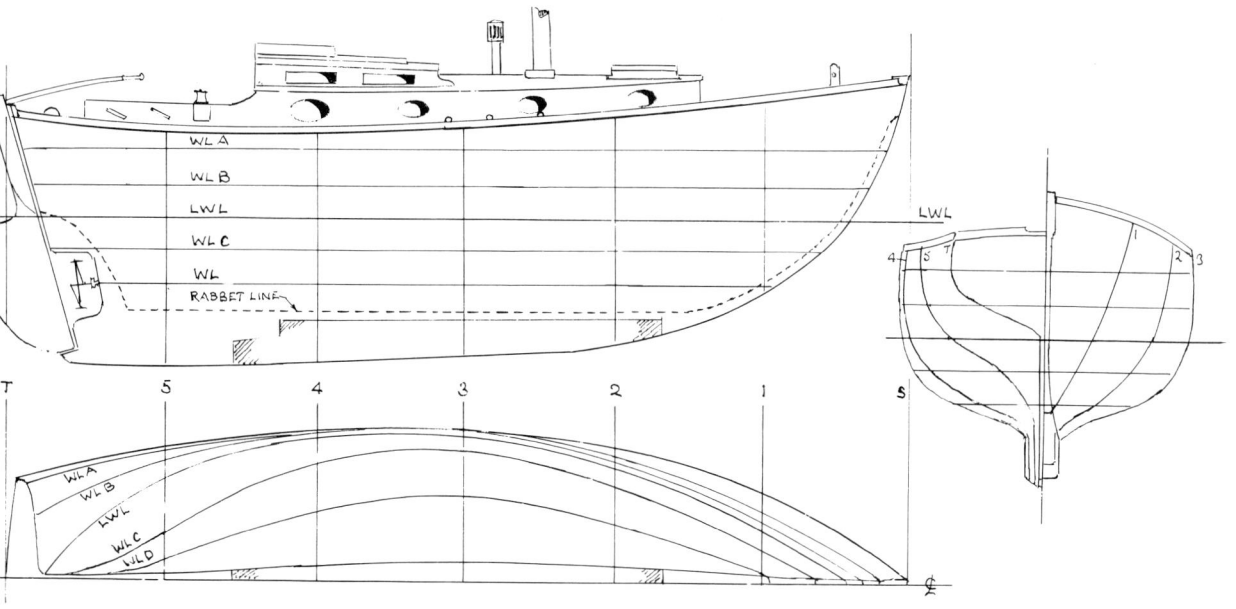

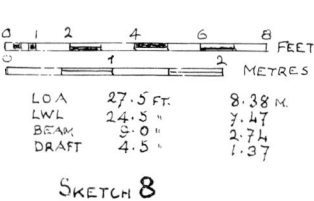

LOA	27.5 FT.	8.38 M.
LWL	24.5 "	7.47
BEAM	9.0 "	2.74
DRAFT	4.5 "	1.37

Sketch 8

all the measurements taken have been metric the usually accepted scale for the plans is 1:20 or 1:10.

If these drawings are to be printed in a magazine or book they should be in black ink (not blue) and with a linear scale of feet/metres added which will be reduced in scale with the drawing to fit the page. Care must be taken to make all lettering and figures on the final drawings neat and clear, and large enough to be decipherable when the whole drawing is reduced to the size required. An optician's reducing glass with reduction about 3:1 is very helpful.

If we want to record the sail plan, the mast, if stepped, is measured with the tape hoisted on the burgee or masthead halyard, and positions of various fittings noted, together with the amount of mast rake at the deck. The boom and its fittings are noted, and any sails to be shown on the sail plan should be laid out flat on a dry floor, as in a boat shed, and measured from cringle to cringle.

The sail plan need not be drawn to the same scale as the hull lines, as it would usually be too large. It can be drawn about half the scale of the other plans, again with its own foot/metre scale drawn in.

For personal use only, to make a model or to carry out alterations to the yacht, the plans could all be drawn freehand; but for greater accuracy or for publication some simple drawing aids will be needed. Unless your ambition is to join the merry band of yacht designers it is not necessary to invest in a complete set of DK ship curves, several varieties of splines or sweeps and a set of shaped lead weights for the splines, nor a planimeter for measuring areas. They can come later if you wish. It is not

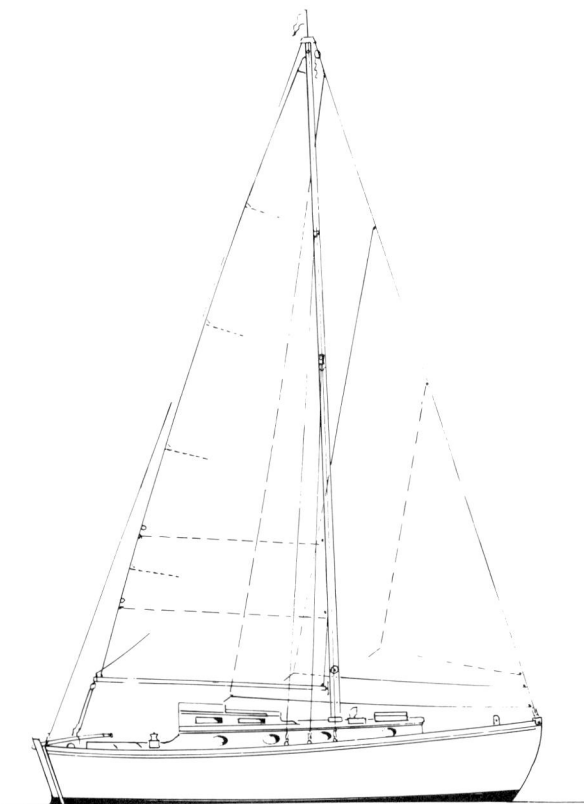

Sketch 9

the quality or complexity of the instruments which controls the accuracy of the drawings, but the natural skill of the draughtsman's hand and eye that matters.

You will need a straight edge rule to measure scale feet/metres, a pair of dividers for pricking off the various points, a 60/30/90-degree set square, a T-square for levelling up, and for fairing in the boat's sections a small flexible curve, say 18in/450mm, which obediently holds its shape after being bent to fit the line. For the longer flowing curves, like the deck plan, the sheer, the waterlines and the keel profile, a flexible steel or thin wooden spline about one metre in length, which bends easily and can be held in position on the drawing with pins or suitably placed weights (anything will do) is all that will be needed by someone with a steady eye.

Since small inaccuracies will inevitably have occurred in the many measurements taken on the spot, however careful the measurer may have been, the spline or flexible curve is unlikely to pass through all the points on the plan at first try: rogue points will lie a little to left and right of the fair curve. They must be adjusted — not the spline or flexible curve forced to conform — until what is clear to the steady eye as a fair curve passes exactly through them all. This is the process described as 'fairing up' and comes with practice.

Your subject, whether a much loved yacht or an interesting type of fishing craft, will now be recorded on paper for posterity, while the budding designer will have had a practical lesson in how to draw and interpret a small vessel's lines.